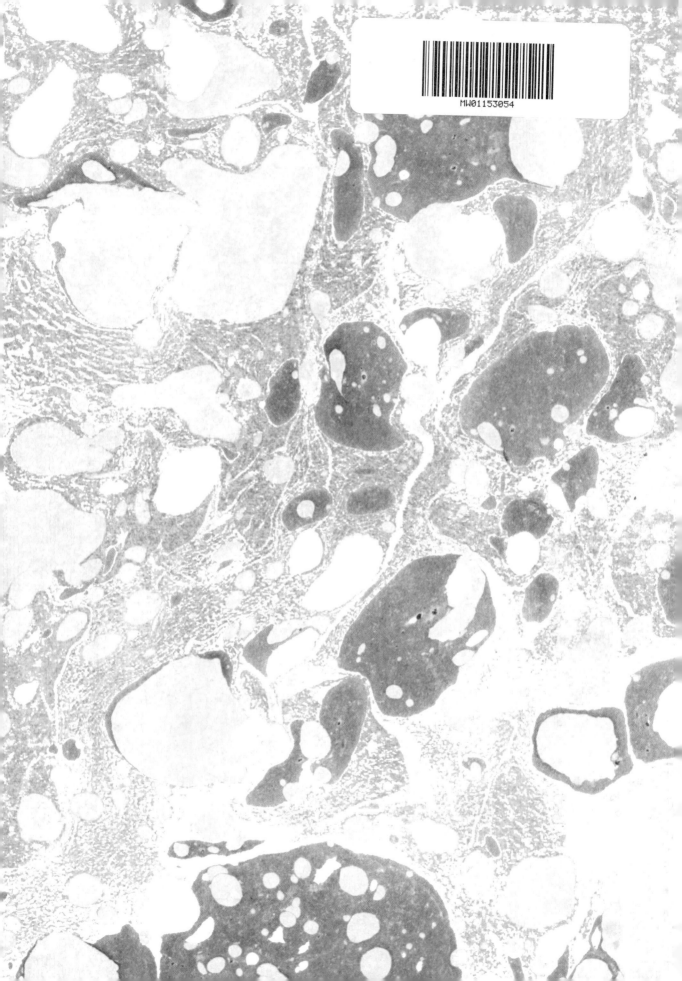

A Velocity of Being

For Stella, Gibson, and Ash.
— Maria Popova

For Elias and Theo, my sisters,
my parents, my friend and mentor Arien Mack,
and the Donnell and Widener libraries,
for sharing the world as it is and as it has been dreamed,
interpreted, imagined, and might be with me.
— Claudia Zoe Bedrick

A Velocity of Being

Letters to
a Young Reader

edited by

Maria Popova and Claudia Zoe Bedrick

ENCHANTED LION BOOKS

NEW YORK

Introduction

By Maria Popova

When asked in a famous questionnaire devised by the great French writer Marcel Proust about his idea of perfect happiness, David Bowie answered simply: "Reading."

Growing up in communist Bulgaria, the daughter of an engineer father and a librarian mother who defected to computer software, I don't recall being much of an early reader—a literary debt I seem to have spent the rest of my life repaying. But some of my happiest memories are of being read to—most deliciously by my grandmother. I remember her reading *Alice's Adventures in Wonderland* to me, long before I was able to appreciate the allegorical genius of this story written by a brilliant logician.

My grandmother, an engineer herself, had and still has an enormous library of classical literature, twentieth-century novels, and—my favorite as a child—various encyclopedias and atlases. But it wasn't until I was older, when she told me about her father, that I came to understand the role of books in her life—not as mere intellectual decoration, but as a vital life force, as "meat and medicine and flame and flight and flower," in the words of the poet Gwendolyn Brooks.

My great-grandfather had been an astronomer and a mathematician who, in the thick of Bulgaria's communist dictatorship, taught himself English by hacking into the suppressed frequency of the BBC World Service and reading smuggled copies of *The Catcher in the Rye*, *Little Women*, *The Grapes of Wrath*, and a whole lot of Dickens and Hemingway. This middle-aged rebel would underline words in red ink, then write their Bulgarian translations or English synonyms in the margins. By the time he was fifty, he had become fluent. When his nine grandchildren were entrusted to his care, he set about passing on his insurgent legacy by teaching them English. When the kids grew hungry during their afternoon walks in the park, he wouldn't hand out the sandwiches until they were able to ask in proper Queen's English.

I never met my great-grandfather—he died days before I was born—but I came to love him through my grandmother's recollections. Around the time when she first began regaling me with them, unbeknownst to me, a young American woman named Claudia—a philosophy graduate student at the New School for Social Research in New York—began visiting libraries and universities across Eastern and Central Europe on various foundation grants as a representative of a Graduate Faculty program designed to support libraries and scholars throughout that region after nearly half a century of intellectual isolation. She visited libraries to talk about the social sciences and humanities, and to learn how local collections worked. She met with librarians—the keepers of the keys—who would show her beautiful illustrated books, illuminated manuscripts, incunabula, and rare journal archives. And she began to seek out picture books from local bookstores, perhaps even some that my grandmother was reading to me at that very time.

Years later, that young woman would become an independent publisher of beautiful, unusual, conceptual children's books—the kind I would go on to celebrate in my own adult life, having transplanted myself from Bulgaria to Brooklyn, in no small part thanks to a life of reading.

And so it was that a package arrived in my Brooklyn mailbox one day, containing three exquisite wordless picture books by a French artist—not "children's" books so much as visual works of philosophy, telling thoughtful and sensitive stories of love, loss, loneliness, and redemption. Enchanted, I looked for the sender and was astonished to find an address in the building next door. Enchanted Lion Books, it said. How perfect, I thought.

The sender's name was Claudia Zoe Bedrick, the publisher. Apparently, we had been working at adjacent studios on the same Brooklyn block. And so Claudia and I finally met, having orbited each other unwittingly for decades, around the shared sun of story and image.

The dawn of our fast friendship was also a peculiar point in culture. Those were the early days of ebooks and the golden age of social media, when the very notion of reading—of intellectual, emotional, and spiritual surrender to a cohesive thread of thought composed by another human being, through which your own interior world can undergo a symphonic transformation—was becoming tattered by the fragment fetishism of the Web. Even those of us who partook in the medium openheartedly and optimistically were beginning to feel the chill of its looming shadow.

Once again, I found myself torn between two worlds—not ideologies as starkly recognizable as the Bulgarian communism of my childhood and the American capitalism of my adulthood, but distinct paradigms nonetheless. I reconciled them—a subjective, personal reconciliation, to be sure—by spending my days reading books, mostly tomes of timeless splendor written long ago by people dead and often forgotten, then writing about them on the Internet, which I came to use as one giant margin for annotating my readings, my thoughts, and my search for meaning. Although I have always been agnostic about the medium of reading—I refuse to believe that reading Aristotle on a tablet or listening to Susan Sontag in an audiobook is necessarily inferior to reading from a printed book—I was beginning to worry, as was Claudia, about what reading itself, as a relationship to one's own mind and not a relationship to the matter of silicon or pulped wood, might look like for the generations to come.

I took solace in a beautiful 1930 essay by Hermann Hesse titled "The Magic of the Book," in which the Nobel laureate argued that no matter how much our technology may evolve, reading will remain an elemental human hunger. Decades before the Internet as we know it existed, Hesse wrote: "We need not fear a future elimination of the book. On the contrary, the more that certain needs for entertainment and education are satisfied through other inventions, the more the book will win back in dignity and authority."

Animated by a shared ardor for that "dignity and authority" of the written word, Claudia and I decided to do something about it—which is, of course, always the only acceptable form of complaint—not by fear-mongering or by waving the moralizing should-wand, but by demonstrating as plainly yet passionately as possible that a life of reading is a richer, nobler, larger, more shimmering life. And what better way of doing that than by inviting people cherished for having such lives—celebrated artists, writers, scientists, and cultural heroes of various stripes—to share their stories and sentiments about how reading shaped them? After all, we read what we are as much as we are what we read.

So began an eight-year adventure of reaching out to some of the people we most admired, inviting each to write a short letter to the young readers of today and tomorrow about how reading sculpted their character and their destiny. We then paired each letter with an illustrator, artist, or graphic designer to bring its message to life visually.

We decided that we would donate all the proceeds from the project to our local New York public library system, because libraries are bastions of democracy and oxygen for the life of the mind, which, as my great-grandfather knew, is our single most ferocious frontier of resistance to inequality and injustice.

Looking back on this labor of love, I am filled with gladness and gratitude for the 121 letters we received—the poetic, the playful, the deeply personal—from contributors as varied as scientists like Jane Goodall and Janna Levin, musicians like Yo-Yo Ma and Amanda Palmer, writers like Jacqueline Woodson and Neil Gaiman, artists like Marina Abramović and Chris Ware, to philosophers, composers, poets, astrophysicists, actors, a 98-year-old Holocaust survivor, Italy's first woman in space, and many more remarkable humans whose splendor of spirit cannot be contained in the shorthand descriptors we often use to condense a person's character and cultural contribution. From these micro-memoirs and reflections by lifelong readers who have made extraordinary lives for themselves emerges a kind of encyclopedia of personhood, an atlas of possibility for the land of being mapped through the land of literature.

Contents

The Letters

Dear Young Reader,

In my memoir, *Brown Girl Dreaming*, I write about "this perfect moment, called Now." I am thinking about this as I lie beside my seven-year-old son, reading to him from a book I at first disliked but have grown to appreciate over the evenings of reading. Two floors up, my thirteen-year-old daughter is supposed to be doing homework but may be checking her Instagram or texting a friend or hopefully snuggled beneath her covers with her own book (*The Absolutely True Diary of A Part-Time Indian* by Sherman Alexie—"Oh my God, Mommy—I love this book SO MUCH!").

It feels like such a short time ago it was her in the crook of my arm, wide-eyed and listening. I impulsively kiss the top of my son's mohawked head (he wants us to let him dye it green—maybe we will—after all, you're only seven once) and he looks up at me, brow furrowed.

"Why are you kissing me in the middle of the sentence?!"

"Because this moment won't always be here," I say.

"Mommy—just read … please."

As the child of a single working mom, I didn't have this moment. There were four of us and at the end of a long workday, my mother was exhausted. Sometimes, my older sister read out loud to all of us and those are some of my deepest memories. *Hans Brinker, or the Silver Skates, The House On Pooh Corner, Harriet the Spy*. While I never read any of those books to my own children—preferring to read from books where their young brown selves were/ are represented on the page—my sister's stories in my ear put me on a journey toward my own stories. I wanted to see myself in books, wanted to know that I existed … fully… out in the world.

The book I am reading to my son is about a troll who is despised in his small town, loves a girl who may or may not love him back. We've just found out the girl is the daughter of Little Red Riding Hood and now the story has my attention—a twist I didn't see coming.

"I don't know why the king is so mean," my son says. "That's not kindness, right Mommy?"

I refrain from kissing the top of his head again and try not to think that this moment of my youngest child beside me, the two of us inside one story, won't always be here. This now is what matters, young reader. The moment we're all living in is what counts—how will this moment, and the stories we're living inside of change us … forever? The smell of my son's hair, his laughter, his whispered "Oh man!" and now, him saying softly "That's not kindness, right Mommy?" This is what reading does. This is what matters most. I smile and turn the page.

Sincerely,
Jacqueline Woodson

Jacqueline Woodson is the author of more than two dozen award-winning books for children and young adults. She was named the Young People's Poet Laureate in 2015 for a two-year term. In 2018, she was named the new National Ambassador for Young People's Literature.

Dear Reader,

Did you ever read a sentence you loved the way you love your favorite animal? My favorite animal is a lioness; how she doesn't have a mane but she always has some blood around her mouth. And how the lionesses work together like good friends when they want to kill something. I've never seen a lioness in person or touched one or slept in the same bushes where a lioness lives, but I've known since I was a little kid that I love them the most.

Sometimes when I'm reading a good book and I'm under a blanket and no one's trying to talk to me, I forget that I'm reading. The tall grass of the story grows up around me, and I'm just another silent creature whose heart beats in that world. If I sit still and keep reading that way, sometimes a sentence stalks by as lovely as a lioness. Blood around its mouth; that fresh, that killer. I read it once, and I know I have to read it again, not look away, watch closely how it moves.

And then I start to notice my eye muscles moving my eyeballs back and forth again, and see the black of the letters on the gray of the page, and I'm just plain reading under a blanket. It's still fun. But the *reason* I read is for the lionesses. For the sentences that pull me in with all their teeth.

Love,
Laura

Laura Brown-Lavoie is writing stories at the library with dirt on her knees. Born, like we all are, of physical labor, of sunlight and rain. Laura's stories are born in a war-waging country, written by a war-hating woman. Her poems grow like weeds from the cracks in the asphalt of Providence streets and get hung upside down in the kitchen to dry.

Dear You,

Yesterday I swallowed a book. Opened it, read it voraciously, then gulped it down in a single sitting. Afterward I sat very, very still, with the book on my lap. I ruminated on the pages I'd dog-eared, the phrases I'd repeated out loud to myself. It made me think—and it made me, and makes me ... me.

My entire life is traced by the books I have read. Books have defined how the world works (sometimes incorrectly,[1] sometimes literally[2]), kept me company,[3] changed my entire career path,[4] and delighted me.[5]

A book, and the universe within, is the touchstone for today, yesterday, and—wow, I can't wait to find out what I read tomorrow.

Bookly yours,
Alexandra Horowitz

1. E.g. *Mouse Tails* by Arnold Lobel. Read at age 4. His mouse runs and runs and runs; wears out his feet; then buys another set of feet from a roadside purveyor. For years I thought feet were replaceable.

2. As a 15 year old I loved reading the dictionary: *Merriam-Webster's 7th Collegiate Dictionary*. I read page upon page, as though it were a suspense story with a hard-to-follow plot. Years later I became a lexicographer (definer of words) at that very dictionary company.

3. E.g. Gabriel Garcia Marquez's fantastic *One Hundred Years of Solitude*, the only English book in Vienna's airport bookstore, traveled with me through Europe when I was 25. I couldn't bear to finish it, because then we would be saying good-bye.

4. That would be the neurologist and writer Oliver Sacks' *The Man Who Mistook His Wife for a Hat*, which combined philosophy and science in a captivating way. Read at age 23. I followed him into that realm.

5. As with Nicholson Baker's fictional *The Mezzanine*, which consists mostly of footnotes. Read at age 20, and many times since. (I suspect you see my inspiration...)

Alexandra Horowitz is a scientist studying dog cognition and the author of several books, including the *New York Times* bestseller, *Inside of a Dog*. She teaches at Barnard College and lives with her husband, son, and two highly sniffy dogs in New York City.

1. The Beatles
2. Kurt Vonnegut
3. Marcello Nizzoli
4. George Orwell
5. Bill Traylor (his blue)

Dear Person Reading This,

A writer can fit a whole world inside a book. Really. You can go there. You can learn things while you are away. You can bring them back to the world you normally live in.

You can look out of another person's eyes, think their thoughts, care about what they care about.

You can fly. You can travel to the stars. You can be a monster or a wizard or a god. You can be a girl. You can be a boy. Books give you worlds of infinite possibility. All you have to do is be interested enough to read that first page...

Somewhere, there is a book written just for you. It will fit your mind like a glove fits your hand. And it's waiting.

Go and look for it.

Neil Gaiman

Neil Gaiman discovered his love of books, reading, and stories by devouring the works of C.S. Lewis, J.R.R. Tolkien, James Branch Cabell, Edgar Allan Poe, Michael Moorcock, Ursula K. Le Guin, Gene Wolfe, and G.K. Chesterson. Now he writes prose, poetry, film, comics, song lyrics, and drama for people of all ages.

Dear Reader,

We wouldn't need books quite so much if everyone around us understood us well. But they don't. Even those who love us get us wrong. They tell us who we are but miss things out. They claim to know what we need, but forget to ask us properly first. They can't understand what we feel—and sometimes, we're unable to tell them, because we don't really understand it ourselves. That's where books come in. They explain us to ourselves and to others, and make us feel less strange, less isolated and less alone. We might have lots of good friends, but even with the best friends in the world, there are things that no one quite gets. That's the moment to turn to books. They are friends waiting for us any time we want them, and they will always speak honestly to us about what really matters. They are the perfect cure for loneliness. They can be our very closest friends.

Yours,
Alain

Alain de Botton is the author of more than fifteen books, including *How Proust Can Change Your Life* and *The Course of Love*. He is also a founder member of The School of Life, a global organization devoted to emotional education, with branches in ten countries.

Dear Reader,

By the time I was in third grade, I knew where to find heroes, monsters, and other worlds between covers, in a friendly little cave with wheels—the bookmobile—which stopped only two blocks from my house. Outside, it looked like an unassuming bus, but inside the walls were lined with colorful books that smelled of wood shavings, silver polish, and dust, just like a real library. It had solid wooden shelves, a card catalogue, and moveable steps for reaching adult volumes. The children's books were shelved at ground level, so I could sit on the carpet and choose among half a dozen to adopt. I especially liked the thin colorful books with gold spines in which Santa rode his sleigh across the sky or Pinocchio danced.

Those portable minds enchanted and befriended me. In some I encountered children who shared my dramas and pains, and they became beloved companions. Clutching a physical book, like holding someone's hand, tenders its own special sensations. I love the comforting weight of a book, and the way your fingers skim across the creamy puddles of its pages, one after another, following the darting minnows of words. You can stroll through a book's compact, neatly bound world, hold it open in both hands, and stare thoughtfully into its face, then close it and see it whole.

No matter where life takes you, you're never alone with a book, which becomes a tutor, a wit, a mind-sharpener, a soulmate, a performer, a sage, a verbal bouquet for a loved one. Books are borrowed minds, and because they capture the soul of a people, they explore and celebrate all it means to be human. Long live their indelible magic.

Yours,
Diane Ackerman

Poet, essayist, and naturalist, **Diane Ackerman** is the author of two dozen works of poetry and nonfiction, including the *New York Times* bestsellers *The Zookeeper's Wife; A Natural History of the Senses;* and *The Human Age*, along with *One Hundred Names for Love*, a Pulitzer Prize finalist.

Dear Children,

I want to share something with you—and that is how much I loved books when I was your age. Of course, back then there was no Internet, no television—we learned everything from printed books. We didn't have much money when I was a child and I couldn't afford new books, so most of what I read came from our library. But I also used to spend hours in a very small second hand book shop. The owner was an old man who never had time to arrange his books properly. They were piled everywhere and I would sit there, surrounded by all that information about everything imaginable. I would save up any money I got for my birthday or doing odd jobs so that I could buy one of those books. Of course, you can look up everything on the Internet now. But there is something very special about a book—the feel of it in your hands and the way it looks on the table by your bed, or nestled in with others in the bookcase.

I loved to read in bed, and after I had to put the lights out I would read under the bedclothes with a torch, always hoping my mother would not come in and find out! I used to read curled up in front of the fire on a cold winter evening. And in the summer I would take my special books up my favorite tree in the garden. My Beech Tree. Up there I read stories of faraway places and I imagined I was there. I especially loved reading about Doctor Doolittle and how he learned to talk to animals. And I read about Tarzan of the Apes. And the more I read, the more I wanted to read.

I was ten years old when I decided I would go to Africa when I grew up to live with animals and write books about them. And that is what I did, eventually. I lived with chimpanzees in Africa and I am still writing books about them and other animals. In fact, I love writing books as much as reading them—I hope you will enjoy reading some of the ones that I have written for you.

Jane Goodall

Dr. Jane Goodall is a primatologist and anthropologist. Her pioneering study of wild chimpanzees in Tanzania, which she began at the age of 26 in 1960, is the world's longest-running continuous wildlife research project. She is the founder of the Jane Goodall Institute, a global community conservation organization, and of the Roots & Shoots program, which engages young people with conservation, and environmental and humanitarian issues.

Dear Reader,

What's so special about books even when you take away the physical? Quite a lot, I think.

1. Books, or these long form thingies, are immutable. You can't go back and change them. Our friend the Interweb is not to be trusted—the electronic world is always in flux, slippery and ever-changing. Our memories are changeable too. The Interweb knows that—and will prey on that aspect of our neuro-haplessness. Book thingies, however, usually remain fixed—with all their faults, quirks, and dated expressions intact. We like books because they stay the same.

2. Books are long. Whether fiction or non-fiction, they create a world that you are immersed in for longer than it takes to read a listicle or even a long magazine article. This immersive experience is what seduces readers and makes them come back for more. A book can be incremental. Dickens, Hemingway, and Twain all wrote in serial form—like podcasts or TV shows. Those episodes sucked readers in and later became classics like *Great Expectations*, *A Farewell to Arms*, and *Pudd'nhead Wilson*.

3. The third reason we like these book thingies is perhaps because we crave a narrative. We like to know that a story or argument is going somewhere, that we can trust the author to get us there eventually (unlike over-stretched TV series), and that each new plot development is considered, purposeful, and not happenstance. Here, then, is a world we can inhabit that has beginnings, middles, and endings unlike the chaotic random place we actually live in. We trust authors—the God-like creators of the universe we step into—to have considered every event as somehow meaningful.

I have a hunch that this trust and love of the safe harbor of structure is why video games will never replace novels. I say that, but maybe we've simply yet to figure out how to maintain that narrative trust while entering a branching structure. Or maybe it's a different kind of pleasure altogether.

So, there is my listicle—3 reasons books are like nothing else—except maybe sometimes like a TV series or a podcast. Ugh. I'm going back to reading my book about how the brain often only sees what it expects to see.

Yours,
David Byrne

David Byrne is a Scottish-born American musician who was the founding member, principal songwriter, lead singer, and guitarist of the Talking Heads. Since then, Byrne has released his own solo recordings and worked with various media including film, photography, opera, fiction, and non-fiction. He has received Oscar, Grammy, and Golden Globe awards and has been inducted into the Rock and Roll Hall of Fame.

Dear Reader,

Much of the time I hate to read. It's the truth. I get impatient.

The information just needs to get in my head fast and reading takes too long. Shouldn't there be a faster way?

After all, letters are just arbitrary squiggles that put together make-up words, which are also arbitrary. (Like why should *chaise* or كرسي or chair mean this thing I'm sitting on?)

And so each arbitrary word is like an elaborate husk that the eyes and brain have to crack open to extract out meaning. It's tedious. Just plug a cable into the back of my head, like Neo. Honestly, I often think this.

But the other day, I was reminded of what we'd lose when the head plug comes along.

I was reading a book to my four year old. It's a book that 52 percent baffles him and 48 percent delights called *Moomintrol, Mymble and Little Mi*. And it's by a Finnish author, Tove Janson, who I am now convinced is a towering genius on the level of Einstein.

Nothing makes logical sense in this book. The characters are always the same, but on page 1 ...

... they wander through a forest.

Page turn. Suddenly they're shooting through the tube of a giant vacuum cleaner.

Page turn. Now they're drinking tea with a hundred electric worms.

Every page turn is whiplash.

The only thing that connects one world to the next besides that Tove Janson thought them up is that she cut holes in every page.

Little wormholes that let you peek forward to the next page. Each page contains a portal.

This simple fact accounts for most of his 48 percent.

But as we turned the pages and slipped through the portals and got to the final page, I thought, he is a new person now. He has passed into his future self.

It occurs to me that every good book is like this. A self-transcending structure. So we read it again.

Yours,
Jad Abumrad

Jad Abumrad created a show called *Radiolab*, which reaches about 1.5 million people a week over radio and is listened to about eight million times a month. He also created a show called *More Perfect*. He tells stories on the radio for a living. And he's a musician.

Dear Reader,

I work a lot in India, where a majority of poor people are illiterate. Here's what one woman in her thirties, a manual laborer, said about the experience of learning to read for the first time: "Whenever I am alone, I sit with the books. If someone behaves badly with me I go home and sit with the books. And my mind becomes better."

Reading opens up worlds inside your head, worlds you can explore, play with, roam around in. Worlds that are in you and that become part of you. When you read, you become bigger. You contain so many emotions and thoughts, so many ideas of what might be, and of what could be better than what is. If you are marginalized or oppressed, insult and denigration are still outside, but they can't force their way in while you are busy inside your own head.

I was not a poor manual laborer. I was a rich well-loved child. What I did not see in my own life was inequality, injustice, people who didn't look like me. Reading novels—Charles Dickens was my great favorite—enlarged my insides so that I had the demand for social justice in my head, even though it was not anywhere in the comfortable world around me.

The great African-American novelist Ralph Ellison said that a novel like his *Invisible Man* could be "a raft of hope, perception, and entertainment" on which America could "negotiate the snags and whirlpools" that stand between us and the democratic ideal. He's referring here to Huck Finn and Jim, who got to know one another as full human beings, rather than just as a white man and a black man, when they traveled down the river on a raft together. On the raft, they had to look at one another, listen to one another's stories. In our divided society, such encounters happen all too seldom in real life, and are fraught with mistrust when they do. Reading can create such encounters in the head, so that the ones that happen in the world are a little less crude, a little less deformed by fear and anger.

Yours,
Martha

Martha Nussbaum is a philosopher and the Ernst Freund Distinguished Service Professor of Law and Ethics at the University of Chicago. She is the author of more than twenty books, including *The Fragility of Goodness*; *Frontiers of Justice*; and *Anger and Forgiveness*.

Dear Readers,

Nearly every book has the same architecture—cover, spine, pages—but you open them onto worlds and gifts far beyond what paper and ink are, and on the inside they are every shape and power. Some books are toolkits you take up to fix things, from the most practical to the most mysterious, from your house to your heart, or to make things, from cakes to ships. Some books are wings. Some are horses that run away with you. Some are parties to which you are invited, full of friends who are there even when you have no friends. In some books you meet one remarkable person; in others a whole group or even a culture. Some books are medicine, bitter but clarifying. Some books are puzzles, mazes, tangles, jungles. Some long books are journeys, and at the end you are not the same person you were at the beginning. Some are handheld lights you can shine on almost anything.

The books of my childhood were bricks, not for throwing but for building. I piled the books around me for protection and withdrew inside their battlements, building a tower in which I escaped my unhappy circumstances. There I lived for many years, in love with books, taking refuge in books, learning from books a strange data-rich out-of-date version of what it means to be human. Books gave me refuge. Or I built refuge out of them, out of these books that were both bricks and magical spells, protective spells I spun around myself. They can be doorways and ships and fortresses for anyone who loves them.

And I grew up to write books, as I'd hoped, so I know that each of them is a gift a writer made for strangers, a gift I've given a few times and received so many times, every day since I was six.

Rebecca Solnit

Writer, historian, and activist, **Rebecca Solnit** is the author of more than twenty books on feminism, western and indigenous history, popular power, social change and insurrection, wandering and walking, hope and disaster, and more. A product of the California public education system from kindergarten to graduate school, she is a columnist at *Harper's*.

Dear Reader,

I was an obedient child. I spent my youth afraid of getting in trouble. (In fact, I am still afraid of getting in trouble.) I was the girl who cleaned erasers during recess. I did extra credit assignments. You would've hated me.

Then one day in 1986, I skipped school. I was a junior at the time, and this was not typical behavior. But I lied to my mother that morning, and didn't get on the bus. I hid. I waited until she left the house for work. Then I snuck back inside, made a giant bowl of popcorn, and curled up with a novel by Ernest Hemingway.

This wasn't a novel I was reading for school; this was a novel I was reading for love. I'd recently discovered Hemingway, and all I wanted was to be alone with *For Whom the Bell Tolls*. And I did manage to spend three perfect hours reading in peace before I got busted. (The school called my mom and reported me.) I paid for my transgression dearly: detentions, grounded, lectures by disappointed parents.

But it was worth it. Those three hours were among the happiest of my life. And they gave me a glimpse into what the future might hold. I realized, "When I'm an adult, I can read whatever I want, whenever I want, and I will always be able to make myself happy."

And that has turned out to be absolutely true.

Thank you, books.

Elizabeth Gilbert

Elizabeth Gilbert was born in Waterbury, Connecticut, in 1969, and grew up on a small family Christmas tree farm. A journalist, novelist, and short story writer, she is the author of several books, including *Pilgrims; The Last American Man; Committed: A Love Story; The Signature of All Things;* and *Eat, Pray, Love.*

Dear Young Friend,

I wish. I wish, I wish, I wish; I wish I were in your shoes now, I wish I were standing where you are standing now, I would swap everything I have learned through my reading, I would swap my entire library of a thousand books, every journey and adventure I have taken through their pages, all the insights about the world and myself, all the laughter, the tragedy, the moments of shock and relief, all the books that have amazed me and that have made me reread them again and again, to be at the beginning as you are, so that I could read them all again for the very first time.

I wish, I wish, I wish I were in your place with all the books of the world waiting patiently for me. It would be so astonishing to come across Coleridge as a perfect stranger and hear his voice for the first time; I would love to know nothing about Shakespeare or Jane Austen, to be overwhelmed by the fact that there is a Rosalind, or an Elizabeth Bennett, or later, an Emily Dickinson, in this world, and then, and then to see my hand for the first time attempting to write even a little like they have, to follow them in shyness and trepidation and beautiful frustration, to walk through the incredible territory we call writing and reading and see it all again with new eyes. I wish, I wish, I wish; I wish I were in your shoes, in a beautiful waiting to know, waiting to read, waiting to write, so that I could open the door and walk through all the books I have ever read or written as if I hadn't. I wish, I wish, I wish; I wish I were in your shoes now.

Yours in anticipation,
David Whyte

The author of many books of poetry and several books of prose, **David Whyte** has traveled extensively, including living and working as a naturalist guide in the Galapagos Islands and leading anthropological and natural history expeditions in the Andes, Amazon, and Himalayas. He grew up with a strong imaginative influence from his Irish mother, among the hills and valleys of his father's Yorkshire.

Dear Reader,

Three generations of my family—my mamá, my children and I—saunter to the library. My mamá's legs have slowed with age. That's okay because it's beautiful out—the kind of numbered day just before fall succumbs to winter.

The neighborhood librarian helps us piece together our haul for the week. My mamá watches, empty-handed. "Don't you want a book?" I say to her.

"I only read important books," she says.

You may have heard the stories. Saturdays were her sacred time to finish what needed to get done around the house. So I learned to love books from watching my late papá. He devoured books, and I wanted to do what he did. I was his shadow.

They say it was because my grandmother died when he was just a baby and never read to him. They say it was because my grandfather was too proud to let him take a scholarship and pulled him out of school. My papá found refuge in books.

They say it was because my abuela was raised by a bandido who didn't teach my abuela how letters made words and never read to her. They say it was because my abuela made my mamá earn her keep so young. My mamá left the books to other people.

So, here we are. We walk home. I smile at my children. They smile back. My darlings love books. They are still young enough to want to do what I do.

We lay out on a blanket on the grass with their father. The sun warms our pages. We gobble them up like fresh-made tortillas. My mamá sits by on the steps with her knitting tote. Things are different now, but I don't argue with her. She is an old powerful devil who does as she pleases. Age has only wised her. As the adage goes: *el diablo sabe mas por viejo que por diablo.*

Then ... my daughter smiles up at my mamá and hands her a book.

Will my mamá read to her? Of course. Doesn't that old devil know? Any book can be "important." My daughter has power too.

All readers have power.

Sincerely,
Claudia

Claudia Guadalupe Martinez grew up in sunny El Paso, Texas, where she learned that letters form words from reading with her father. She now lives in Chicago and has authored various books for young people, including *The Smell of Old Lady Perfume* and *Pig Park*, both published by Cinco Puntos Press.

Dear Reader of Tomorrow (and Today),

When I was your age I had an agreement with my mother: Whenever she went shopping, she left me at a bookstore or a library. Wherever we were in the world, that was our arrangement, and it made us both happy. As a result, I didn't complain about how long it took her to shop, ever. If anything, when she came to get me, even though I loved her, I was a little sad.

They called me a bookworm when I was your age. I taught myself to read and walk at the same time so I could read more while I walked to school. My mother was always telling me I was going to ruin my eyes by reading so much but I am still the only one in my family who doesn't need glasses—it may be I even strengthened my eyes.

I started reading so much back then because we had just moved to Maine and I had wanted us to stay in Guam. Maine seemed hard, cold and hopeless compared to the beautiful South Pacific island with warm seas and colorful fish that we had left behind. And while there was no way for me to return, in books I found doors to other worlds besides the one around me—and many other lives. Pretty soon, I was sneaking away to read, and it was because each of these books I loved felt like a present left behind for me by a stranger who somehow knew exactly how I felt.

I learned, gradually, to love Maine as much as Guam. But I read now for the same I reasons I read then—to feel less alone. But I read for more than that: Reading teaches me the answers to problems I haven't had yet, or to problems I didn't even know how to describe. And when I feel less alone with what troubles me, it is easier to find solutions. A book to me is like a friend, a shelter, advice, an argument with someone who cares enough to argue with me for a better answer than the one we both already have. Books aren't just a door to another world—each book is part of a door to the whole world, a door that always has more behind it. Which is why I still can't think of anything I'd rather do more than read.

Yours truly,
Alexander Chee

Alexander Chee is the author of the novels *Edinburgh* and *The Queen of the Night*. He has taught writing at Wesleyan University, Amherst College, the University of Iowa Writers' Workshop, Columbia University, Sarah Lawrence College and the University of Texas – Austin. He currently lives in New York City, where he curates the *Dear Reader* series at the Ace Hotel.

Dear Person-Who-Is-Afraid-Of-Books,

Don't forget: You don't have to finish every book you start. When I first started reading, I was always a little bit afraid of the books I was opening, because I felt like I had to finish them no matter what, and maybe I wouldn't understand what was inside. And I'd be trapped. But books aren't like a plate of vegetables that you're supposed to eat because they're good for you. Books are like an enormous ice cream sundae the size of a mountain. You can eat as much of a book as you want and when you're full or start to feel disgusting, you can put the book down and walk away. But you don't have to finish every book!

Love,
Your Friend Amanda

Amanda Palmer is a writer of books and songs and tweets and blogs, and a player of the ukulele and the piano, and a person who stands on tables and sings for strangers, and a mother, and someone who doesn't finish a lot of the books she starts. She used to be one of those street performers who dressed up like a statue. Really!

Dear Children, Young as You, Old as We,

Reading can be the gateway to dreams fulfilled, to ideas for life's progress. Stirring your imagination, it offers insight into yourself and maybe the selves of your family, friends, teachers, authorities, even adversaries, players for other teams. In books you'll find landscapes you long for or learn to run from. Truth and its consequences could stare at you. Victory can be presented vividly, delightfully, hauntingly. Shared reading (at bedtime, in classrooms, by a campfire) brings us closer to one another. Our own experiences, emotions, visions—so alike, so different—encourage mutual responses through the well-written word.

My novelist husband, William Styron, declared it was not the prose but the created character that is remembered. He thought about Flaubert's Madame Bovary as he developed (and listened to) his Sophie.

Often the only child at home, I began to read at four. Books were my pals, my inspiration. It is never too early or too late to start exploring. *A Child's Garden of Verses* kept time in my head as I swung in our sycamore tree in Baltimore. Bertram's funny animals and Terhune's fiercer ones (how I longed to meet a grizzly!) stayed with me in the yard until the lamplighter came by. At dawn I walked the yellow brick road to Oz with Dorothy and her wondrous companions.

By six I was grounded in other realities. I pulled down books from my parents' shelves—Kipling, Millay, Tagore—I believed I understood. Then I settled into typical schoolgirlhood, plotting to be detective Nancy Drew, or traveler Beverly Gray, Susannah of the Royal Mounties. By eleven and twelve I reincarnated as Scarlett O'Hara, Anna Karenina, Madam Curie, and by my teens—obsessed with newspapers—pilot Amelia Earhart and, most deeply, Eleanor Roosevelt. What lives I led!

Men, fictional and real, were my heroes, too, of course. Hemingway's, Fitzgerald's, and later Salinger's guys stole my heart as did poets Yeats and Eliot. May they and their successors steal yours.

Sincerely,
Rose Styron

Rose Styron is a poet, journalist, and human rights activist. Her work has appeared in *The Nation*, *The New Republic*, *American Poetry Review*, *The Paris Review*, *Ms. Magazine*, *Vogue*, *Ramparts*, *The New York Times*, and more. In 1970, she joined the founding group of Amnesty International USA and has since served on the board of numerous NGOs.

My Dear Future Friend,

I will probably never know you. We may not ever walk this earth at the same moment. But listen carefully. Books saved my life. In the stillness of reading, the silence save for the sandpapery sound of my fingers turning the page, I was born. In the quiet of a summer afternoon spent in a hammock, of a winter night spent sneaking under the covers with a flashlight, dawned the awareness, slow but unmistakable, that I was not alone. That I was not insane. That my heart was not so very different from everyone else's. Books made me feel less ashamed. Less weird. Less different. They connected me deeply to my own humanity.

Books did this for me. They don't glow. They don't beep. They don't link to anything else. You can't surf them. Or click on them. They may seem simple—even boring—at first. You might wonder: well, what do they do? What's in it for me? After all, we're talking about a primitive pile of pages, taking up space. Words—just words! They line up, one after the other, scratches of black on white. They gather dust on shelves that might otherwise display sea shells, or blown glass, or photos of family vacations. But keep them close, my young friend. Keep them within reach, always. They contain nothing less than the entire world. Opulent. Staggering. Rich beyond your imagining. Waiting for you to crack it open.

Dani Shapiro

Dani Shapiro is the author of four memoirs—*Still Writing*; *Devotion*; *Slow Motion*; and *Hourglass*—as well as several novels, including *Black & White* and *Family History*. Dani lives with her family in Litchfield County, Connecticut.

Dear Reader,

When I was 12, I was given a scholarship to a private girls' school in the town where I lived. All the other girls came from another—wealthier—town. They were driven to school in Jaguars and Mercedes Benzes. They ate artichokes! No way would I ever fit in.

In the midst of my funk, the English teacher assigned *A Member of the Wedding* by Carson McCullers. As it happens, Frankie, the book's heroine, is also 12 and also wants to belong. Her yearning is such that she wants to know everyone in the world and for everyone to know her—exactly what I wanted! That's what stunned me, not just the intensity of the longing, but the specificity. It meant—it had to mean—there were other people in the world like me. Not just Frankie, a fictional character, but the author who had to have felt that way herself in order to give Frankie that longing. I felt such an intimate connection with her, as if she'd looked deep inside me and knew me in the way I wanted the world to know me. Reading didn't just offer escape; it offered connection!

All these years later, I just have to look at my copy of *A Member of the Wedding* on my bookshelf to experience again how I felt when I first read it and to feel the full force of that connection: to Frankie, to Carson McCullers, to the 12-year-old I was and to 12-year-olds everywhere.

Yours,
Emily

Emily Levine uses humor to show how big ideas from science permeate and shape our institutions, our everyday lives, even our relationships. She began her career in improv, made her way as a stand-up comic, then as a TV writer/producer, before—finally!—marrying her brain and her funny bone to become a philosopher/comedian. As the writer and star of the movie *Emily @ the Edge of Chaos*, she brings that calling into full bloom.

Dear Spacetime Traveler,

For each foot away you hold
a book, you see
a billionth of a second
back in time.

Hold the pages close.

They are portals
to worlds that exist,
as surely as the heavens hang
with planets beyond our own.

The tactile bending of
pages or pixels
conjure lives just as human
as any you have known.

Step forward if you're brave.

Stories become our
well-worn pathways,
and our companions, too.

Repeat them and release them,
so that their truth may one day
come back to you.

Space travel is easy
what's hard is
telling fiction from the truth.

Lucianne Walkowicz

Lucianne Walkowicz is an astronomer and an artist. In her scientific work, she studies stellar magnetic activity and how stars influence a planet's suitability as a host for alien life. As an artist, she works in a variety of media, from oil paint to sound. In 2017, she was appointed Chair of Astrobiology at the Library of Congress.

Dear Future & Present,

We have some strange sayings in the English language. I've spent some time reading quotes, proverbs, and aphorisms from people all over the world. The sayings can deliver powerful life lessons in beautiful language. Like this one, which is my favorite: "If we stand tall, it's because we stand on the shoulders of our ancestors." That's a West-African proverb. No one knows its exact origin but sayings tell a great deal about what a people hold dear. I tend to think this saying would never gain popularity in the US, or anywhere in the Western world without a massive cultural shift. Think about it. The myth of the all-powerful individual who succeeds on sheer will alone is so prevalent here that the idea that people you've never seen could be responsible for your good fortune would seem ridiculous. But in some places it's normal for ancestors to be celebrated, and there it wouldn't be a stretch to imagine that those long gone people on the other side might be rooting for you to succeed here on this side.

One of the oddest American sayings is: "Curiosity killed the cat." What does it mean when a culture says this? It means stay in your place. Keep your head down. Don't ask questions. Stick with what you know. If it's different, leave it alone. It means don't cross the border. Don't color outside the lines. Stay put because wherever your curiosity takes you could be dangerous.

Here to the rescue come books, with their covers and pages beckoning. "Bring your curiosity. It's welcome here." Books show us people who pray another way, speak a language we haven't heard, wear clothing and hairstyles we've never imagined, eat food we don't see in our supermarkets. And books show us all we have in common, surrounding us with community we didn't know we needed. Showing us there is no "other." Books let us know we're not the center of the universe; the universe has many centers.

I looked up "curiosity." It means: a desire to know and learn. Inquisitive. An old meaning is: accomplished with skill or ingenuity. For my ancestors in this country, a desire to know and learn often meant punishment or even death. Maybe curiosity did kill the cat, but the spirit of who I am and who we are has never died. In fact, it's contained in something my mother says. If someone tells her "curiosity killed the cat" she responds "satisfaction brought him back."

If my ancestors weren't curious in the oldest sense of the word, I certainly wouldn't be here. So my advice to you is the same I give my daughters: Keep asking questions. Color outside the lines. Draw your own pictures. Draw your own maps. Create your own legends.

I wish you joy on your quest.

One,
Mariahadessa Ekere Tallie

Mariahadessa Ekere Tallie is the author of *Strut*; *Dear Continuum: Letters to a Poet Crafting Liberation*; and *Karma's Footsteps*. She has performed poetry and taught in the United States, Namibia, the Netherlands, Belgium, and England. Her work is the subject of the film, *I Leave My Colors Everywhere*. Ekere is the mother of three galaxies who look like daughters.

Dear Friend,

Could you imagine a world without access to reading, to learning, to books?

At twenty-one, I was forced into Poland's WWII ghetto, where being caught reading anything forbidden by the Nazis meant, at best, hard labor; at worst, death.

There, I conducted a clandestine school offering Jewish children a chance at the essential education denied them by their captors. But I soon came to feel that teaching these sensitive young souls Latin and mathematics was cheating them of something far more essential—what they needed wasn't dry information but hope, the kind that comes from being transported into a dream-world of possibility.

One day, as if guessing my thoughts, one girl beseeched me: "Could you please *tell* us a book, please?"

I had spent the previous night reading *Gone with the Wind*—one of a few smuggled books circulated among trustworthy people via an underground channel, on their word of honor to read only at night, in secret. No one was allowed to keep a book longer than one night—that way, if reported, the book would have already changed hands by the time the searchers came.

I had read *Gone with the Wind* from dusk until dawn and it still illuminated my own dream-world, so I invited these young dreamers to join me. As I "told" them the book, they shared the loves and trials of Rhett Butler and Scarlett O'Hara, of Ashley and Melanie Wilkes. For that magical hour, we had escaped into a world not of murder but of manners and hospitality. All the children's faces had grown animated with new vitality.

A knock at the door shattered our shared dream-world. As the class silently exited, a pale green-eyed girl turned to me with a tearful smile: "Thank you so very much for this journey into another world. Could we please do it again, soon?" I promised we would, although I doubted we'd have many more chances. She put her arms around me and I whispered, "So long, Scarlett." "I think I'd rather be Melanie," she answered, "although Scarlett must have been so much more beautiful!"

As events in the ghetto took their course, most of my fellow dreamers fell victim to the Nazis. Of the twenty-two pupils in my secret school, only four survived the Holocaust.

The pale green-eyed girl was one of them.

Many years later, I was finally able to locate her and we met in New York. One of my life's greatest rewards will remain the memory of our meeting, when she introduced me to her husband as "the source of my hopes and my dreams in times of total deprivation and dehumanization."

There are times when dreams sustain us more than facts. To read a book and surrender to a story is to keep our very humanity alive.

Sincerely,
Helen Fagin

Helen Fagin was born in Radomsko, Poland, in 1918. During the Holocaust, she and her sisters secured false papers for themselves, which kept them alive until liberation. Helen immigrated to the United States, taught herself English, and eventually became a professor at the University of Miami. Later, she was invited by President Clinton to serve on the advisory board for the WWII memorial in Washington, D.C.

Dear Reader,

I want to tell you that everything will be okay.
I want to tell you that it will get better.
I want to tell you that it all works out in the end.
But sometimes it doesn't.

Most times it is hard and we usually end up getting used to it. But there is something you can do in response: read.

Read until your heart breaks and you can't stand it anymore. Read until you have paper cuts from turning pages or blisters from swiping a screen.

You see, here's the thing: even at their worst, books won't abandon you. If they make you cry it's only because they are *that* good.

You can depend on books. They will always be there for you. Their patience is infinite and they have been known to save lives. They can help you become a smarter, more interesting person. Books can probably help you get dates, though I don't recommend you ask that much of them too often (you don't want to limit their power).

Books—like dogs—are among a handful of things on this planet that just want to be loved. And they will love you back, generously and selflessly, requiring very little in return—until they are complete, their light and their wisdom and their hearts sputtering to an inevitable, lonely end.

Debbie Millman

Debbie Millman is a designer, artist, educator, and the host of *Design Matters*—one of the very first podcasts ever. She also chairs the world's first Master's Degree program in Branding at the School of Visual Arts in New York City and has written several books on design and branding.

Dear You,

Reading saved me.

When I was twelve, I spent most of my day trying to be invisible. The year before I'd been the new girl in school, and I'd spent a lot of time trying to be accepted. Trying to have friends. I don't have to tell you how hard that is. Belonging is some magical mix that no one can manufacture. The very desire to bend and twist to fit in—assures your rejection. They did not like me. They hated me.

I spent a lot of time alone. I rode the bus alone, I spent weekends alone, I ate lunch alone. Except I was never alone. I always had a book in my hand. And if you have a book in your hand, you are not alone. If you have a book, you don't need to bend and twist to fit—you're there. You are in. You crack the spine and you are a welcome member of the group.

I didn't eat lunch alone, I ate lunch in Castle Rock, Maine, with Stephen King. I've hung out with Jane Austen. I've curled up in corners with Toni Morrison. I've climbed trees with Louisa May Alcott. With a book in my hand, I was transported. I wasn't twelve years old in Illinois. I was 90 in Nigeria or 15 in India. I was the Emperor of China. I was Harry Potter. I was James Bond. I was in Wonderland. I was in a Little House on the Prairie.

Books are how I met Anne Frank and Malcolm X. How I became a spy, a ballerina, an astronaut, several Queens of England, a girl on fire. Books are how Boo Radley, a spider named Charlotte, a bear named Pooh and I all became good friends.

If you read a book, you are never alone. You can go anywhere. Be anyone. Do anything. If you read a book, you will be all right. Even if you only read one book. Even if you read the same book over and over. Inside that book is a whole world. Inside that book, you have friends waiting for you. Inside that book is sanctuary.

If you have a book in your hand, you can stop being invisible. Because you're a little more invincible.

At least that's how it was—and still is—for me.

Happy Reading,
Shonda Rhimes

Shonda Rhimes is a screenwriter, director, and producer. She is the first African-American woman to create and executive produce a top ten network series, the medical drama *Grey's Anatomy*. Her other shows include *Private Practice*; *Scandal*; and *How to Get Away with Murder*.

Hello Reader,

Though we've never met, we already have a lot in common. We're both human beings, which may seem obvious—but our shared humanity is hard for most people to keep in mind. Because you read, and because you are reading this right now, you know more about me than almost anyone else I've come across today: the woman who handed me my coffee at the place I go on Orchard Street, the people I passed on the sidewalk when I ran out for eggs, the ticket-taker at the movie theater up on Houston, and the security guard at my office building in Union Square. In Manhattan, you are alone even when you're surrounded. I am sure you know what I mean.

Did anyone I met today take the time to see me? Maybe they found a little bit of themselves in the lion and lamb tattooed colorfully across my hands, or the grey speckling of my beard. Maybe they heard a faint accent in my speech, imprints of my childhood in the South and industrial Midwest and it reminded them of someone else—a childhood sweetheart or a summer camp friend from a long time ago. If they're readers like you and me, than they're used to searching for connections with strangers. They're easy to find when you make a practice of opening a good book and opening your mind to another person. We readers do that. We welcome the thoughts and feelings of someone else right into our brains, and we find ourselves in what resonates. We see that everyone is part of the human condition, even and especially us.

Reading is for the brave among us. It teaches us how to love people we don't know and will probably never meet. It teaches us that we too deserve that same sort of love. That faith is, in fact, the work of being a fully realized person.

So thanks for reading and please don't ever stop.

Your friend,
Thomas Page McBee

Thomas Page McBee is the author of *Amateur* and the memoir *Man Alive*, a LAMBDA-award winner, as well as a best book of 2014 for *Publishers Weekly*, *Kirkus Reviews*, *NPR Books*, and *Buzzfeed*. His writing and reportage on gender have appeared in *The New York Times*, *Playboy*, *VICE*, *The Rumpus*, and *Pacific Standard*. He lives mostly in Brooklyn.

To the Children of Tomorrow,

March 12, 2014

I don't know exactly when this letter will be read. "Tomorrow" could be a very very long time from now. So I will imagine that "tomorrow" is March 12, 2114, because I cannot imagine anything further in the future than a century.

First of all, hello! I hope that you are doing well. I would guess that you have computer chips implanted in your brains and are directly connected to the Internet. So, you have instant access to vast amounts of information, books, and the thoughts of other people, all constantly flowing into your neurochip. I hope that you are able to stop this flow when you want. Everyone needs quiet time with their own thoughts. Even today, in 2014, when we use computers outside of our bodies to connect to the Internet, there is far too much information to digest. We can be suffocated by it. We have to be choosy about what information we put on our plate. I hope you can do the same.

Keep in mind that information is not the same as knowledge. You still need to think about what you are learning and what it means. To do that, you will need to turn off your neurochip from time to time. It is valuable to connect to the world, and it is also valuable to disconnect and listen to your own mind think.

Alan Lightman

Alan Lightman is a physicist, novelist, essayist, and educator. He has taught at Harvard and MIT, where he was the first person to receive a dual faculty appointment in science and the humanities. He was born in Memphis and lives near Boston.

Dear You,

You can't remember being born, or the moment you first laughed, yet these episodes live inside you as vital contributors to the anthology of your inner self. Every good and bad experience leaves a rubbing inside you; an imprint of feeling whose impact doesn't require memory or articulation to matter. Your deepest self is a mural of feeling-patterns running down your veins, across your heart, and they shrink or expand correspondent to your attention, nourishment and empathy. Books send signals from their feeling-patterns to yours, teaching you to identify what you've not been able to name. Follow their flares.

Just like you, a book has an interior life, and just like you it only ever wants to be known; each of your efforts to connect freshens your best traces. Through a book, an author offers her own painted pulses, trusting you'll care, and hoping you'll recognize its match inside you. To accept something meaningful from a stranger you'd never ask for in person is a privilege as rare to receive as to extend. Every reader should behave like a book, pushing others toward growth, aiming to deepen the most enduring relationship: the one we have with ourselves.

Your friend in Brooklyn,
Amanda

Amanda Stern was born and raised in Greenwich Village. She is the author of *The Long Haul*; *Little Panic*; and eleven books for children under pseudonyms. In 2003, she founded the Happy Ending Music & Reading Series, which ran every month at Joe's Pub through May, 2016.

To A DEAR READER

49¢

Who, me?

Yes, you!

Pretty much everyone learns how to read when he or she is a kid in school.

cat
hat
mat

2×
3+
8-

You have to learn to read in order to survive.

ACME CHOCOLATE SYRUP

ACME MOTOR OIL

DO NOT PUSH THIS BUTTON ↓ — EVER

FREE CUTE PUPPIES! CALL TIMMY

BRIDGE OUT

HOW TO USE YOUR NEW TOASTER

STOP

There's also homework-type reading:

If Sally bought three pencils, and Joe bought six pencils, and Bob bought one pencil, and Nan...

That's not the kind of reading I'm talking about. I'm talking about **REAL** reading.

Different people get absorbed by different things...

Soccer Cooking Knitting Pirates
Stamps Romance Flying Shells
Ants Birds Saucers
Art History Dogs
Fashion

It's the same with books. You have to find the ones that float your boat.

SADDLE UP!

THE BIG BOOK OF PONIES

PRANCER OF BRIGHT CANYON

NEIGH!

HORSE-O-PALOOZA

When you find a book, you love, it's like being able to travel without having to buy tickets or carry a suitcase or get shots.

You can venture to dangerous exotic places—

or see what it's like to live in a completely different era.

A great book lets you see the world through the eyes of an infinite number of people.

It's like watching a movie in your head.

The outside world becomes irrelevant.

You don't have to be the strongest or the prettiest or the smartest person in the world.

All you need is a terrific book, your imagination and a good place to read.

Who knows? Maybe someday, you'll write a story of your own.

ROZ CHAST

Dear One,

When I was very young, knowing how to read was my secret superpower. Nobody expected a pre-pre-pre-schooler to read, so grownups underestimated me. They would spell words they didn't want the children to understand. I understood. They used big words so the children wouldn't know what they were talking about. I went to the dictionary.

I loved to read! I read constantly, so my vocabulary was always expanding. More words, more power.

I didn't know it at the time, but reading was helping me become a real person. I usually felt like the property of the grownups who bossed me around and told me what to think and what to believe. The more I read, the more I became myself, an individual with ideas.

Reading gave me the ability to roam around the printed page and explore other people's experiences. I could learn about different ways of thinking and behaving. When I had big questions about life, I would read until I found answers that made sense to me. I learned how to decide what was true for me.

All these years later, I still read to find answers to my biggest questions in life and to decide what's true for me.

Reading has been my favorite thing to do since I learned how to do it.

As long as I can read, I can unlock the secrets of the world.

It's my best superpower.

Hoping it's your superpower too,
Ruth Ann

Ruth Ann Harnisch invests in intersectional social change through philanthropy, equities, and venture capital. Following a career in journalism, she founded the Harnisch Foundation, which supports people and organizations working to advance equality and inclusivity. She is also the producer of *Icarus*, winner of the 2108 Academy Award for Documentary, and is a certified professional coach and a volunteer crisis counselor on the Crisis Text Line.

ART BY **CHLOE BONFIELD**

Dear Future Humans,

Reading hijacks your mind better than a virtual reality headset ever could. It doesn't just present a story to your senses—it injects the action right into your mind. Books can't dazzle your eyes or roar in your ears or make your tongue swell with sour. But they can leave parts of themselves behind in your thoughts.

A book reaches you by using mind control, but only with your consent. You are in charge of translating the words into visions, sounds and smells. That's why the story in a book becomes yours, like a memory that you were lucky enough to gain without experience. Its wisdom can be yours, too, or its terror, love, adventure and chaos.

I guess what I'm trying to say is that picking up a book is like plugging in a game controller that drives your brain. It gives you a lot of power. It fills you with adrenaline. Oh, and by the way—the 3D graphics processor in your brain is pretty great, too. Once you start using it, you won't ever want to stop.

Love,
Annalee

Annalee Newitz is editor-at-large at Ars Technica, and the founder of the science/science fiction blog io9.com. She is also the author of *Scatter, Adapt, and Remember: How Humans Will Survive a Mass Extinction*, and the novel *Autonomous*. She has a Ph.D. in English and American Studies from UC Berkeley, and was the recipient of a Knight Science Journalism Fellowship at MIT.

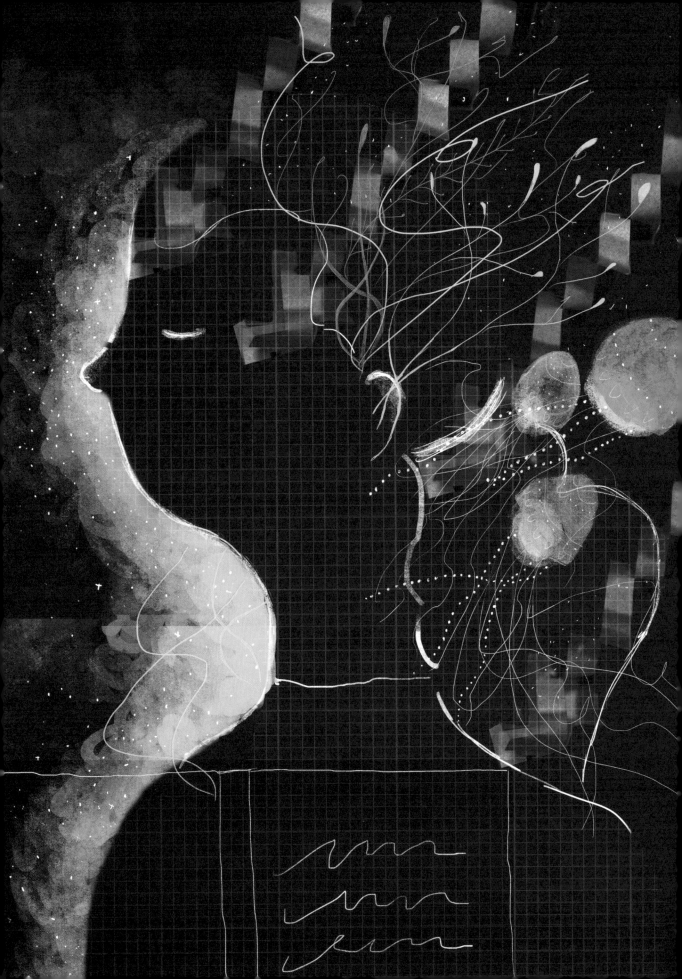

Dear Ones,

Reading changed my life. Writing saved it.

I can't promise writing will save your life, though learning to express yourself can go a long way. But I can promise reading will change your life for the better. You'll be smarter, savvier, you'll have a way to connect with people of all ages, and you'll never be bored. What could be better?

Love,
Judy

Judy Blume spent her childhood in Elizabeth, New Jersey, making up stories inside her head. She has spent her adult years in many places doing the same thing, only now she writes her stories down on paper. Judy and her husband George Cooper live on islands up and down the East Coast. They have three grown children and one grandchild.

Decur

Dear Young Reader,

I am sitting, on this summer afternoon, in my favorite reading place under
the black cherry tree on the hill, looking out over the fields. In the moment
before I open a book I like to just hold it between my palms and remember
what an amazing thing it is, a meeting of tree gifts and human gifts on the
same page. A place where the reader and the writer meet in reciprocity to
create something which has never existed before. A book is an invitation to see
the world through another's eyes: blue eyes, black eyes, fiery green wolf eyes.

It feels like the tree is reading over my shoulder, sharing the stories, as
it has every right to do, since they are printed on a sheet made of tree cells.
Books let us be like trees, don't you think? Seeing beyond the span of our own
lives, reaching high into the sunlight and deep into the dark fertile soil of
imagination. They let us play in their branches or dream in a hammock. If we're
lucky our minds will widen with every volume, like growth rings of wisdom.
And books attract more books, more ideas—like bright singing birds flocking
to a tree of knowledge.

Splat! It's raining cherry juice from overhead, dripping ripe summer onto
my paper. Maybe the tree is writing to you, too, in its own particular shade of
purple ink. Did you know that the first ink was probably berry juice? The first
book written on tree bark? Maybe we're witnessing the start of a great forest
novel written in a crazy code of drips and drops, a symbiosis between tree and
human. What meaning would they make? Every being has a story, whether we
know how to read it yet or not. We should learn. Trees writing? Is it any more
magical than the fact that these inky tracks we call letters prancing like ant
footprints across the page can carry us away with the stories they tell? What
story will you tell, in your own particular shade of ink?

Robin Wall Kimmerer

Robin Wall Kimmerer is a mother, a botanist, a writer, and a grateful student of plants. She is the author of *Gathering Moss* and *Braiding Sweetgrass*. A member of the Citizen Potawatomi Nation, she lives on an old farm in upstate New York, tending cultivated and wild gardens.

Dear Reader,

All novels are science fiction. Every time you read a novel, it seems as though you can know what someone else is thinking—like you can experience another person's internal mental state.

The truth is that no human being has ever known what any other human being was thinking, ever, in the entire history of our species.

Telepathy is, alas, not real.

But in novels, it is. The fact that novels are so compelling—the fact that we can weep for imaginary people who never lived and never will live—says something about how we experience other people.

The way you know who your friends are, the way you know how to apologize, the way you know how to get your parents to let you stay up for an extra 20 minutes, is that you have models of those people running in a little simulator in the back of your mind.

That simulator is full of real people, imaginary people, dead people, even partial people. When a friend says, "Have you seen the new kid? She's really mean, watch out," your simulator starts up a new model, with a sign over its head reading "new kid" and a mean expression on its face.

This is where prejudice and love both come from. Training, mastering and interrogating our simulators is how we learn empathy and get along with others.

And novels are an exciting and weird way to give the simulator a workout—by creating the illusion of telepathy.

Cory Doctorow

Cory Doctorow is a science fiction author, activist, and journalist. He is co-editor of *Boing Boing* and the author of many books, including *Walkaway*, a novel for adults; *In Real Life*, a graphic novel; *Information Doesn't Want to Be Free*, a book about earning a living in the Internet age; *Little Brother*, a young adult novel, and its sequel, *Homeland*.

Dearest You, Co-Author, Planet, Reader of Meteorites,

Because it takes time for even light to travel the distances of our universe, the starlight we see now is from the past. The star sometimes called the North Star, for example, is so far away that when we look up into its single eye we are witnessing light emitted hundreds of years ago. There is even a star nicknamed Icarus whose light, astronomers have calculated, reaches us from 9 billion breathtaking light-years away.

A sentence, even this one, is, in a way, like starlight. It reaches us from a past & we stand a moment in its messages. But a sentence doesn't just reach & change us, we also change it. See: I am writing this sentence now (April 20th, 2018), on a day that, by the time you read this, will have already passed. Kids & birds are shouting in the schoolyard. Sparrows are sharing the bread. & you, dear reader, are reading these words on some future day, carrying the text with the breath of your body. Perhaps as you read, someone is cooking garlic & onions in the pot, or rain is falling loudly down onto your abuelita's garden. The sentence is a time machine, giving us access to one another's presents & histories. For example, if I say "My Adey Zuphan lived with her chicken atop a hill in Emba Derho," I might picture my grandmother's sister with shining eyes, alone except for her chicken in a hudmo atop a hill. But you might picture your own beloved grandmother who lives not atop a hill but in a basement apartment, with one cat & a very old television. Suddenly you are filling the verbs & page with what you know. & just like that, we become each other's co-makers. With each new reader, the sentence becomes a new version of itself. & so the world.

      *

In the Sudan, 2008, an asteroid exploded over the Nubian Desert. It was dawn. Several people saw a flash of light in the sky just after morning prayers.

A band of Searchers searched the desert for some trace of a sky-fallen thing.

What did they imagine as they looked? Jewel-like, iridescent space tears? Perhaps finding something inside? A tiger, a sleeping peony bush, kerars. The voice of Mos Def singing about the moon.

However farfetched, reader, you are the one who helps this dreaming to live a moment in the sunlight of your mind. &, speaking of sunlight, the Searchers did eventually find meteorites in the desert. & when scientists studied them, they discovered that those "rocks" were remnants of a lost planet. & inside of some, they found diamonds.

A text is a trail of its writer's imagination. It is the remnant of one planet being found by another (you).

& if there are diamonds here, dear reader, it is because you made them.

                                               *,
                                           Aracelis

Aracelis Girmay is the author of the poetry collections *Teeth*; *Kingdom Animalia*; and *The Black Maria*, as well as the picture book, *Changing, Changing*. Originally from Southern California, where the street names of Orange, Cherry, Bristol, Flower, and Lime were a kind of poetry, she now lives and reads with her family in Brooklyn, New York.

Dear Reader of Tomorrow,

I realize that you departed on your journey and have been on the road a few days (to you, it may seem like years). You've probably traipsed long miles through the forest, you've made a good group of friends, and you know the colors and names of plants and birds. At this point, you'll discover that the world is vast and surprising, marvelous and terrible ... you'll discover a lot of things. But, I want to let you know that at some point along the road you will end up in a scary place. Don't be afraid of it. When you get there, it's understandable that you may want to stop and catch your breath. Do it! Drink some water, breathe deeply ... and prepare to face whatever it is!

You will have arrived at a point on the road where an enormous obstacle looms in front of you, a huge, terrible question [drum roll]:

What is the meaning of life, after all? (She with eyes wide open will ask.)

Stay calm. You will decide what to do. You can always evade the question, go around it, even pretend you've never seen it (if you're good at pretending, the road will open up to you as if by magic). What I recommend, though, is that you look the question in the eye. And if you're the brave soul that I think you are, you will!

In that moment, perhaps a bit concerned, you'll think: How do I take on such a mountainous question? One so high that snow glistens at the top?

Don't worry. Soon you'll discover that there are trails, stairs, and passages to help you, and you can always choose the paths that you like best. However, there is an amazing route to scale the mountains of questions. Not all travelers know that route, and it's one that I'd like to share with you: books.

Books are of great help because they contain the voices of so many other explorers and mountain-climbers. They are the ones who can point out the best trails and reveal the most secret passages. So if you want to stare the enormous question in the eye, you'll be glad you brought some books in your backpack.

This is the message I want to leave for you.

You'll do great.

And don't forget: like the highest peaks in the world, questions love to be scaled and conquered. Don't pass them by.

Um abraço,
Isabel

Isabel Minhós Martins was born in Lisbon in 1974. Words—what we can do with words and what words can do with us—were always her favorite mystery. She graduated in Communication Design from Lisbon College of Fine Arts and after some work for advertizing agencies, she and three friends founded the publishing house Planeta Tangerina.

Great Places to Read Books

It's lovely to read in the bathtub
(but be careful the book doesn't slip)!
You can read while you sit in a door frame
(but don't cause someone to trip)!

You can read while under the covers
(with the help of a secret flashlight).
You can climb up a tree and read there
(as long as you're not scared of heights)!

You can read in a tent if you're camping
(or out in the woods on a hike).
Or read while you sip hot cocoa
(by a fireplace if you'd like).

You can read on a bus or a subway
(but make sure you don't miss your stop)!
You can read while you swing in a hammock
(but don't swing too hard or you'll plop)!

You can read while you lounge in a beach chair
(wear an SPF that is strong).
You can read while you sit on a toilet
(but don't stay there too long)!

You can read by yourself in silence,
or read out loud with a friend.
You can go see your local librarian,
and ask what books they'd recommend!

Sarah Kay

Sarah Kay is a New Yorker, a poetry writer and reader, a playwright, a songwriter, a postcard lover, the daughter of a Taoist mother and Brooklynese father, and the founder and co-director of Project VOICE—a group dedicated to using spoken word poetry to entertain, educate, empower, and inspire.

Hey,

Are the eggs of the purple unicorn edible?

It's a fair question, and one worth discussing. If they are edible, would you be willing to have a unicorn-egg omelet? Would that be fair or right or even delicious?

The thing about reading is that anything is possible. No special effects, no stunt men. If the writer can write it, it's real.

And the other thing about reading is that it will take you somewhere impossible, without a teacher or a parent going there first.

Discovering what's possible is your job. And there's no better way to do your job than reading something new.

Go make a ruckus,
Seth

P.S. Comic books are okay too.

Seth Godin is the author of more than fifteen books, including *Linchpin; Tribes; The Dip;* and *Purple Cow.* His books have been translated into more than 35 languages. He writes about the post-industrial revolution, the way ideas spread, marketing, quitting, leadership, and most of all, changing everything.

hello!
My name is Ariel and I want to tell you about the time I discovered the cartoonist R. Crumb and how it changed my life.

I was 12 years old and obsessed with comics. I loved newspaper strips like "Calvin + Hobbes" and "For Better or For Worse" and comic books like Disney's "Uncle Scrooge." My dad also loved comics and kept his collection from when he was young on a shelf in his office.

Sometimes he would take down some of his old "Little Lulu", "Donald Duck", or "Plastic Man" comics from the 1960s to let me read. One day, my dad wasn't home, but I really wanted to read his comics. I snuck into his office and used a chair to climb up and reach the shelf.

please don't fall

It was then I learned my dad had many comics I'd never seen before, including some intriguing ones by someone named R. Crumb. I began looking through an R. Crumb comic called "Zap" and, like the drawing of the man on the cover, felt a shock of electricity run through me.

The comic was gritty, dirty, funny, obscene, and flat out weird. It was as if R. Crumb himself had exploded onto the page. Some of the drawings were "adult", as in, too sexual for a 12 year old, and while this certainly gave me the thrill of looking at something I knew I probably shouldn't, what was truly

exciting was realizing the potential of what comics could be. They could be your darkest fears, they could be your most bizarre desires, they could be the things you're afraid to say out loud.

They could be you.

I carefully put the R. Crumb comic back so my dad wouldn't be able to tell I'd touched it...

... but I walked out of the room different.

I soon began writing my own comics with one goal in mind: to be as honest and raw and true as I could, and give other people the feeling that those R. Crumb comics gave me.

Ariel schrag

2015

Dear Reader,

Teachers and other adults too will tell you a lot of things you may argue with eventually—you may well have your own different ideas, and perhaps better ones. But about the importance of learning to write and read, easily and fluently, you will never argue. Such wonderful people will speak to you—to YOU—from the pages. Such adventures you will have through their telling, that you would never otherwise have! And all because the words on the page are not a puzzle but a door to many worlds. To write is delight, to read is to plant the seed of endless excitement. I promise you.

Yours,
Mary Oliver

Mary Oliver published her first book of poetry in 1963 at the age of 28. Her poetry collections include *American Primitive; A Thousand Mornings; Dog Songs;* and *Blue Horses.* A recipient of the Pulitzer Prize and the National Book Award, Oliver was born in Ohio and spent half a century in Provincetown, Massachusetts, with her partner, Molly Malone Cook, before moving to Florida.

marc johns

Dear Person,

Why read?

Because you only have one life but reading gives you many lives. Because you only have one personality but when you read a book you can be inside another mind and heart. Because experiencing elegance of language is one of the greatest pleasures of consciousness. Reading lets you be quiet in a chaotic world and commune with amazing people who may happen to be dead now, so not too easy to connect with otherwise. Reading startles you. Reading upsets you. Reading takes apart your world and expectations and rearranges them. Imagine the last few years without the books you have loved—it would be a much flatter, sadder experience of living. We read as a form of faith.

Naomi Wolf

Naomi Wolf is an author, journalist, feminist, and former political advisor to Al Gore and Bill Clinton. After the success of her first book, *The Beauty Myth*, she became a leading spokeswoman for the third-wave feminist movement. Her subsequent books include *The End of America: Letter of Warning to a Young Patriot* and *Vagina: A New Biography*.

Dear Fellow Reader,

A book is a boat. It is a wide, dry, warm boat that you can sail swiftly across the ocean, or perhaps it is a big steamer that moves at a majestic pace across the sea. You can see everything from the deck—the whole world, in fact.

A book is an airplane. You will step on board and fly, soaring anywhere and everywhere, traveling to every corner of the earth, while sitting in your reading chair.

A book is an x-ray machine. You will open up your book and suddenly be able to do the most amazing thing: you will be able to see inside people. You will be able to read their minds and hear their private thoughts and imagine what it feels like to be inside their heads. There is nothing else in the world that can give you that power.

A book is a soft blanket. It will wrap itself around you, keeping you cozy and comfortable. Books sometimes can make you laugh, and sometimes they can make you sad, but they will always hold you close.

A book is an adventure. In a book, you will do battle, climb peaks, perform experiments, fall in love, find treasure, make magic. You will learn remarkable things. You will be able to time-travel—within a book, you can visit every part of history, and you can even visit the time before time. You simply can't imagine what you'll experience in the pages of a book because there are no limits at all. None!

A book is a dream, something that takes place in a different dimension, where nothing follows the rules of ordinary life. Can animals talk? In a book, they can. Do kids run the world? In a book, they often do. Whatever you can dream of, a book can explore with you.

A book is a friend forever and ever.

Yours,
Susan

Born in Cleveland, Ohio, **Susan Orlean** is a journalist and the author of numerous books, including *The Orchid Thief*. She has been a staff writer at *The New Yorker* since 1992.

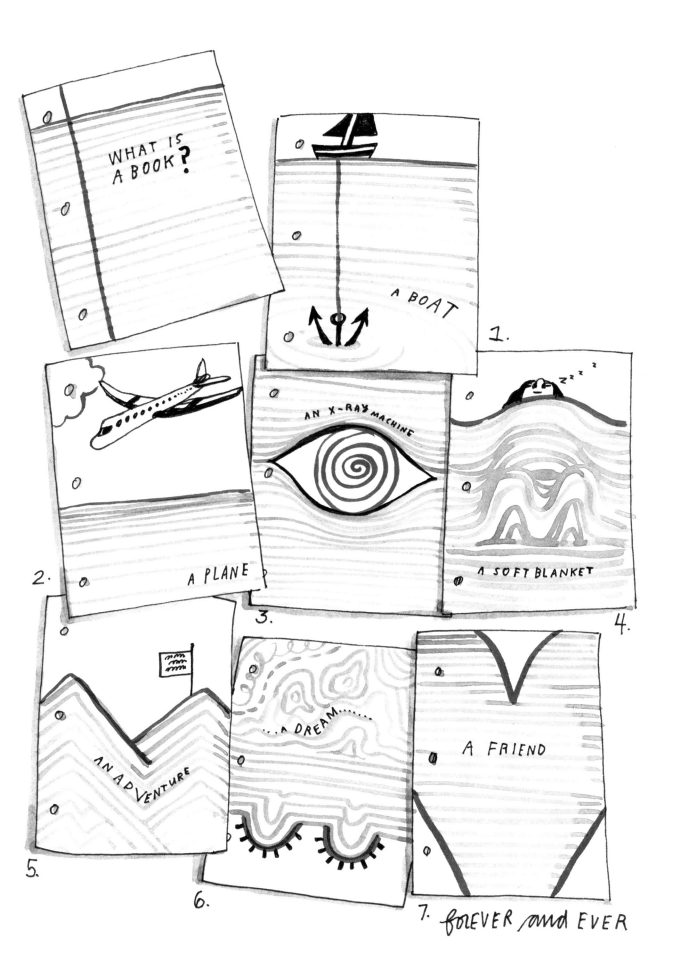

Dear Future Children,

When I was a kid my two favorite books were *The Wizard of Oz* and *The Lion, the Witch, and the Wardrobe.* They told exciting, sometimes funny stories, but what I liked best was the idea that strange, magical worlds might be so close at hand you could accidentally stumble into one the way kids in the books did—just on the other side of a closet or, at most, a short tornado ride away.

I was jealous of Dorothy and Lucy. *I* wanted to find a magic portal. *I* wanted to fall into a magical world. When I opened a closet, I wanted to feel a chill and find snow falling behind the coats. When I opened my front door, I wanted to see a yellow brick road winding off towards the Emerald City, though I would have settled for any vista that wasn't my own boring street.   You can guess what happened: nothing. I'm grown up now and I never walked through a door and found myself anywhere but in the next room or the front yard. All the closets I know have backs. I never met a witch or a wizard. I never made friends with a talking lion. I won't lie: I'm disappointed. I'm also mad I never got to live on the moon, but that's a different story.

Here's the consolation prize: I now realize that the books themselves were the magic portals. I know that sounds corny, and I'd probably roll my eyes if I was you, but it's true. And not just the Oz and Narnia books. *Any* good book takes you to new places, puts you in other people's shoes, sends you off on an adventure, makes you believe whatever is happening on the page is real, at least while you're reading it. And that's the best kind of magic I know of.

Not that I've given up on "real" magic. Here's a secret I've never told anyone before: even though I'm old enough to be a grandfather—a *young* grandfather— I still sometimes hope or pretend I'll find a strange new world inside a closet or maybe at the end of a long tunnel, when I'm in a car. Or maybe even in my own refrigerator—why not?—in the back there, behind that crusty old jar of mustard ... Is that a little door, or window?

Nope. Just a stain.

Yours,
Bruce

Bruce Handy is the author of *Wild Things: The Joy of Reading Children's Literature as an Adult.* He is also a contributing editor at *Vanity Fair*, a frequent contributor to the *New York Times Book Review*, and managing editor at *Esquire*.

Dear Children,

    The world itself is all beautiful, but sometimes it can be hard to see that, and books let you understand moments of beauty you might otherwise miss.

    Daily life is hilarious, and books will help you find that humor and laugh out loud at life. This will help you to keep on living.

    We are all alone in some ways, and books make us less alone. The writers who write them reach out from their imagination and experience into yours. You need never be lonely again.

    The arc of the moral universe bends toward justice, but sometimes you need books to show you how to bend toward justice yourself.

    Human beings are fundamentally absurd, and nothing shows off that absurdity better than a book. A sense of the absurd is good armor for life.

    It's hard to follow the golden rule and be kind to others all the time, but books will show you how to do it. They can make you kinder; they can make other people kinder to you.

    Reality can get dismal. Nothing will do a better job of rescuing you from reality than a book; it is as good a means of escape as your own boat or rocket ship.

    Sometimes, it's good to feel sad. Books will make you melancholy when you need to be melancholy. If you've lost something or someone, books will help you feel your own feelings about loss.

    Sometimes, a book can confer happiness on you. Sometimes, the ideas and emotions that a book pins down are just the ones you need to wake yourself up into joy.

    All the books in ours and many other languages are made from the juxtaposition of twenty-six shapes. There is nothing else so exquisitely versatile in all of creation. It's a wonderment to behold those shapes in action.

    Please read, and please write.

All my love,
Andrew

Andrew Solomon is a writer and lecturer on psychology, politics, and the arts; a winner of the National Book Award; and an activist in LGBT rights, mental health, and the arts.

Dear Book Lover,

Let me take you on an adventure. We're not going by plane, train or spaceship—instead we're staying right here on this page. These words can provide you with the greatest adventure of all time, if you let your imagination run free.

I've seen the world in all its glory. I've crossed the globe by plane, sped through stunning landscapes on trains, sailed the high seas by boat, and skimmed some of the world's tallest peaks in a balloon. And with Virgin Galactic I hope to gaze back on Earth from space. But before I was able to do all this, I learned as a child that adventure doesn't have to be physical.

Some of my biggest and most exciting escapades have sprung from the pages of books. I've journeyed into the frozen heart of Antarctica with Robert Falcon Scott; experienced the courage of the troops on the battlefields of Stalingrad; walked the Long Walk to Freedom with Nelson Mandela; spent long summer days sailing on the Swallow and the Amazon; and let the wild rumpus begin *Where the Wild Things Are.*

Reading broadens the mind, heightens the senses, and enlivens the spirit. It gives us hope, drive and inspiration. Make it a habit, give it unrestricted access to your imagination, and you will be presented with opportunities and possibilities beyond your wildest dreams. As one of my favorite authors, Dr. Seuss, wrote, *Oh, the Places You'll Go!*

Imagination is one of humanity's greatest qualities—without it the world would be a very dull place. Let the words of a book guide your imagination, and the spirit of adventure motivate you to set goals, push yourself, thrive in the face of hardship, and achieve epic feats.

And when you do get the opportunity to travel, take a book with you. Books can be wonderful teachers, saviors during wait times, and companions on the road. Plus, they often hold memories of where you have been, recalling experiences and emotions of times spent exploring.

Read and choose your own adventure, and the whole world will be yours, at the ends of your fingertips.

Yours,
Richard

Richard Branson is an entrepreneur and businessman. In 1972, he opened a small record shop called Virgin Records, which has since transformed into Virgin Group, a multinational conglomerate of more than 400 companies. A keen adventurer, Branson has sailed across the Atlantic and crossed oceans in a hot air balloon.

Dear Young Explorer,

Books are my friends. They open doors to new worlds and introduce me to a fascinating array of new people—heroes and villains, girls and boys to whom I felt closer when I was little than to many of the kids at my school, men and women who teach me about places, feelings, and myself. When I was young they were my escape from reality, a way to live somewhere else whenever I didn't want to be in a car or a bus or a game that I was bad at. Today they are still my haven, the little place I go to relax every night when I get into bed and let the cares of the day fall away from me. And they go on forever. You can never read them all; there will always be wonderful new stories to explore, people to know and places to visit. They are like video games that you can never ever get to the end of, but so much better, because you imagine what the assassin sneaking up on the castle looks like, and how the wind sounds through the trees or the waves on the shore. You are the programmer, not just the player. If you learn to love books, you will never be lonely. You will always have something to look forward to at the end of the day, first thing in the morning, on a trip, at the beach, or anywhere else you can read. And even if all the power goes off, as long as the sun comes up in the morning, you can still read.

Yours truly,
Anne-Marie

Anne-Marie Slaughter is President and CEO of New America. She was the director of policy planning in the U.S. Department of State from 2009 to 2011. She is the author of many books, including *Unfinished Business: Women Men Work Family*.

Dear You,

Sometimes big ugly stuff happens to the people you love and running away doesn't really work. Sadness follows you around like a hungry dog who won't leave you alone till you pay attention to it.

I was three years old when my dad was diagnosed with cancer. He came home from the hospital with just one leg. A few years later, he lost his other knee—and by "lost," I don't mean that he couldn't find it; I mean that a doctor operated on him and took it out and replaced it with a metal one. After that, other doctors beamed radiation at his neck and back to blast the cancer and gave him drugs that made him so sick he pulled the car over once so he could puke into a stranger's front yard. But the cancer kept coming back anyway and every time it did, we had to say goodbye again, just in case. His body, eventually covered neck-to-knee in scars, looked like a map of the world.

And it kind of was.

When my dad realized that he wouldn't live long enough to show me the *actual* world, he got busy giving it to me in books—books he wanted me to read then and books he wanted me to read in the future. There were books about Mexico and Alaska, natural history books, books by Annie Dillard, Wallace Stegner, Louise Erdrich, books on fishing and others on knots, even books about other books. Books were talismans my dad hoped would protect me when he couldn't do it himself anymore.

I still keep one of his favorites, *The Year of the Whale,* on a shelf above my desk. It's a story about a mother sperm whale and her calf and how they survived the long, dangerous journey from Hawaii to the Arctic, navigating by the stars.

Years after my dad died, I became a writer myself. I was working on my own book about animals when I learned that it's not just the mother whales who protect the calves—the fathers do too. Sometimes a male will carry a calf gently in his mouth if she's tired or scared, letting her go only when she's ready to brave the waves and the cool dark depths on her own.

The best books are like that—and my dad knew it. They pick you up when you're frightened, teach you what you need to know, and then set you back down again when you're ready.

Love,
Laurel

Laurel Braitman is an author, historian, and anthropologist of science. She holds a Ph.D. in Science, Technology, and Society from MIT and is a Senior TED Fellow. She is the author of *Animal Madness*. She lives on a houseboat in Sausalito, California, with her dog, Cedar.

Dear Friend,

May I share a memory from when I was little?

One afternoon, I was sitting on my mother's lap, reading out loud from a book about a young prince. There came a moment in the story where the prince began to sing, so naturally I looked at the words on the page and started to sing. My mother was surprised by the new melody I had created: "Where did you find that tune?" she asked. I pointed at the text on the page and said, "It's right there." At that age I imagined that everyone reading this would hear the same melody that I was singing. But I was inventing music! Little did I know that I would grow up to be a composer and that making music would become my livelihood and my joy.

Now let me share another story that I cherish from my upbringing; a more distant one. 1400 years ago in the deserts of Arabia, a meditative prophet named Mohammed had a vision of the Angel Gabriel who came to him with a message: "Read"... or, in the original Arabic: " اقرأ ." This was the first word of the Quran.

In the years following the prophet's death, his followers built an empire where they contributed to every branch of knowledge, from algebra to optics and medicine to music. Countless things we have today would not exist without their contributions: that includes space stations, glasses, aspirin, your iPad.

They were able to do this because they were inspired to seek out the power that comes with being able to read. You deserve the same power: to have your imagination unleashed and be carried across the galaxy in the space of a sentence. Read! Whether your path is to build an empire or to find the lifelong companionship of music, every path is possible with that power. It all begins with one word; the same word that was delivered to an ancient prophet on the wings of an archangel: اقرأ.

May peace be upon you

عليكم السلام

Mohammed Fairouz

Mohammed Fairouz is a composer exploring geopolitical and philosophical themes. A New York City native, he volunteers at the LGBT Community Center every Sunday.

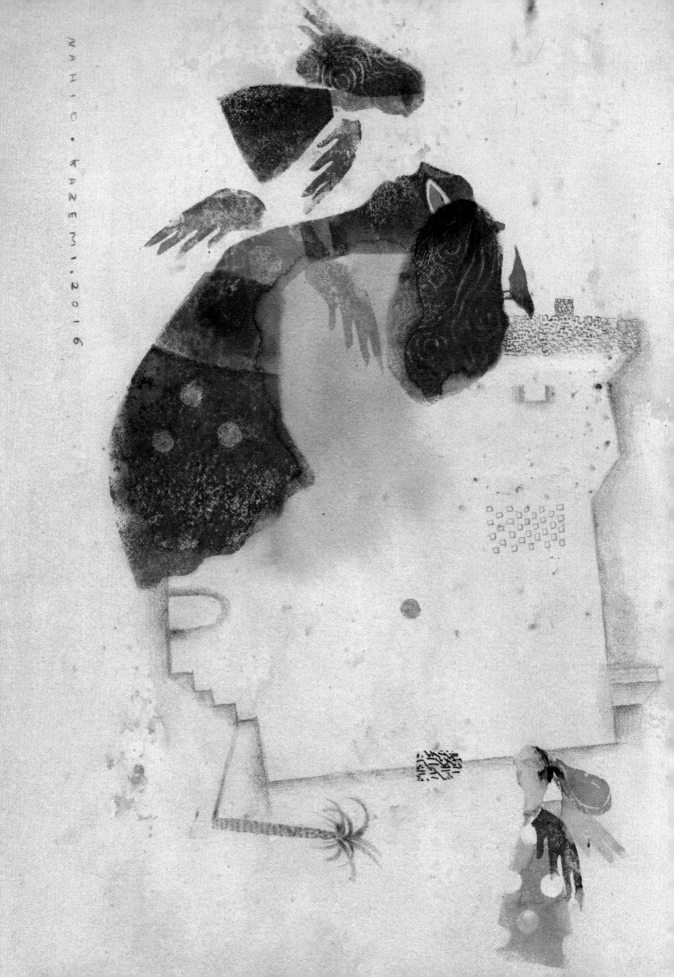

To a Reader,

The book whispers to you
From the shelf in a small voice,
   Reader, into the tiniest

Shell of your innermost ear
So quiet you might mistake it
   For silence

But once it comes to rest
In the nest of your hands
   The book is a bird

And though you never know
If or when, a flapping
   May happen—

You remain in your bed
Yet there you soar over
   Whistling mountains:

The hidden wooden cabin
Is for you to explore, that
   Train traverses

The valley of your mind
And the kid on the fence
   With a bucket of milk...

Across the still white lake
A single spider slides on
   Six little roller skates.

The roller skates are yours,
Your listening makes them
   Spin and when wings

Close again you are back
But you still feel a shiver,
   Adventurer.

   Matthew Burgess

Matthew Burgess is an assistant professor at Brooklyn College. He is the author of *Enormous Smallness: A Story of E. E. Cummings* and *Dream Closet*.

To the Open Minds of Tomorrow,

To read is to play.

To read is to participate in a lie.

To read is to open a channel in your brain. A passageway where you welcome foreign neurons to branch out and tickle the fabric of your mind.

To read is to expose a vulnerability, for at least a brief moment, to surrender to another perspective, to bring it inside yourself and try it on.

To read is to adventure with a sorcerer, able to conjure dreams which can only be completed by your own imagination.

To read is to experience collections of pure thought, simultaneously so well-defined and descriptive, yet almost infinitely abstract.

To read is to push upon the boundaries of human consciousness.

To read is to be alone.

To read is to be together.

To read is to stand naked in the cold and scream "What do you got?"

To read is a skill, a blessing, an invitation, an opportunity.

Go forth, use your eyes, your brains, your hearts.

Godspeed,
Aaron

Aaron Koblin is a pioneering digital media artist, best known for his data-driven crowdsourced art works around visualization. The founder of Google's Data Arts Team, he is the recipient of the Smithsonian Cooper Hewitt National Design Award, an Emmy award, and two Grammy nominations. His work is in the Museum of Modern Art, the Centre Pompidou, and the Victoria and Albert Museum, among others.

Dear Reader,

I love diving under the waves of the ocean. In fact, I've spent thousands of hours over many years swimming with the fish, seals, whales, corals, dolphins and other magnificent creatures in the deep blue.

Would you like to guess my favorite animal? It's not the otter, though they are playful. And it's not the pelican, though its soaring figure is majestic above the ocean horizon. And it's not the blue whale, though its size takes my breath away. No, my favorite animal doesn't live under the waves. My favorite animal is you and me. Humans.

Now, humans don't have the best reputation under the waves these days. We are taking too many fish out of the ocean and dumping our trash into it. It's nasty business and it needs to change.

But humans are still my favorite, because we have an insatiable appetite to learn. And by learning about the ocean, we are learning to care about its future. And through caring, my great hope is that we will act to protect the ocean and the creatures in it. They do need our help.

By reading, we can explore deep oceans, meet exotic animals and learn about the great systems of life on our planet. That's amazing! Our cavemen ancestors certainly didn't have this luxury. So try reading a book or two about the ocean. You may be surprised what you learn. It could change your life, as it did mine. And if you're curious enough—and I hope you will be!—one day you'll join me in a dive underneath the waves.

A library isn't just a collection of books. It's a portal to anywhere you want to go in the universe. Go explore!

Dr. Sylvia Earle

An oceanographer, explorer, and conservationist, **Sylvia Earle** pioneered the use of modern SCUBA gear and the development of deep-sea submersibles. She has led more than 50 expeditions, has spent more than 7,000 hours underwater, and set the world record for the deepest untethered dive. Dr. Earle is the founder of Mission Blue— a global coalition advocating for the creation of a worldwide network of marine protected areas.

Hello!

This is your Brain! Can you hear me? <Tap tap>

We're together a lot, and I always have a lot on my mind (Haha a joke!) but I wanted to pause and say:

Thank you for taking care of me with the books you read.

When I was lonely, you introduced me to characters who were smart and adventurous and who I felt could be my friends.

When I was confused, you found books that explained it all, and I got to learn new things. So I didn't have to feel as embarrassed about not knowing.

When I was sad, you picked up comics and funny stories that made me laugh. (I especially like fart jokes and flying robots. For future reference.)

When I was angry, you chose stories of heroes and love and sacrifice, and I realized that there were problems bigger than mine to get upset about in the world. So I didn't feel as angry anymore.

And when I was bored, you took me places I'd never been, allowed me to learn about people I'd never heard of, and all of it made me thirsty for more!

There are so many books to choose from, but no matter what we read together, afterwards, I don't feel quite as trapped inside of you, my human container. I can't wait to see what you find next!

In conclusion, not to get sappy, ahem, but …

I'm very glad that we are going to be together forever.

Love,
Your Brain

Felicia Day is the star, writer, and producer of the original web series *The Guild*, a show loosely based on her life as a gamer. She co-starred in Joss Whedon's Internet musical *Dr. Horrible's Sing-Along Blog*, and has appeared in numerous TV shows and films, including both *Supernatural* and *Eureka*. She runs the YouTube channel *Geek & Sundry*.

Hey Kids,

I want to tell you something interesting about reading books. It's that books are about possible worlds—not just the worlds we know well. They goad us to go beyond the familiar, to consider not just the here-and-now but the might-be. And that makes the world bigger and bigger and more and more interesting. Also, books don't require that we do anything beyond imagining the world they're telling about, and that's the kind of imagining that's really fascinating! And then, maybe some day, you might even want to write a book, not just read one—to set out your own ideas about what kinds of worlds are possible! How about that?

Yours,
Jerome Bruner

Jerome Bruner lived more than 100 years. Born blind, he wore thick glasses after doctors restored his sight. A wise, gentle teacher, Bruner believed that children construct their worlds the way he did before he could see. Our minds determine much of what we perceive, he taught, and children can learn more than grown-ups think they can; story-telling, not logic, is the key. Jerry loved boats, Paris, Ireland, and children.

Dear Girl,

Don't put it down.
Your book, that is.
Keep a flashlight by the bed and keep reading once your parents say goodnight.
Learn how to walk and read at the same time.
Put an actually interesting book inside your very boring math textbook and read away.
Hold your book outside the stream of the shower so you can read while you scrub, and don't bother washing your reading hand.
If your grandmother says, "No reading at the dinner table!" you just say, "Reading is scientifically proven to strengthen your mind and multiply your brain cells and keep you alive forever! You should try it Grandma! Jeez."
If your father says, "Be social," say, "I have plenty of friends inside this book." Then start a book club.
You see, you have something very special. A clubhouse. A cave. A horse you can ride anywhere. A restaurant that always has a table for you. A massive universe where you are the brightest star, floating by a swirl of other stars. Reading is your place: you will always be able to return there. So, dear girl.
Don't put it down.

Lena Dunham

Oberlin graduate and New York City native, **Lena Dunham** is the creator, writer, and star of the HBO series *Girls*, for which she received numerous Emmy nominations and two Golden Globes. In 2015, she and Jennifer Konner founded *Lenny Letter*, a weekly online feminist newsletter.

Dear Friend,

Once upon a time there was an ordinary little girl named Miranda who lived in an ordinary house in an ordinary town. One day she looked in her mirror and said, "I'm tired of everything! I'm tired of *me!* I *hate* being ordinary!"

A voice behind her said, "Then open me."

Miranda turned around and saw a book on her desk. "Did you say something?" she asked the book politely.

"I said, open me!"

So Miranda opened the book and started reading a story about a sailor, a ship's captain, and a whale. It was so interesting that she read for a whole hour.

Then the book said, "Close your eyes, turn around, and look in the mirror again."

So Miranda turned around and looked in the mirror with her eyes shut tight, and she saw a creature with three heads: the head of a sailor, the head of the ship's captain, and the head of the whale.

"Oh, my!" she cried. "What has happened to me? How strange and wonderful I am!"

"Now open your eyes," the book said. So Miranda opened her eyes and she saw herself again—only she no longer looked ordinary. She looked strange and wonderful, too.

"You see?" the book said. "We are *all* strange and wonderful. And whenever you doubt it, just open a book. You will become somebody else—and that somebody else will be a part of you forevermore."

"I understand," said Miranda. Then she opened the book and started reading again.

Sincerely yours,
Terry Teachout

Terry Teachout is a critic, biographer, librettist, author, playwright, and blogger. He is the drama critic at *The Wall Street Journal* and critic-at-large at *Commentary*. One of the first arts bloggers on the Internet, he blogs at *About Last Night*, and is the author of *Duke: A Life of Duke Ellington* and *Pops: A Life of Louis Armstrong*.

Dear Potential Readers of the Future in an Increasingly Distracted Era,

My father doesn't give advice. I have gleaned from my friends over the years that many fathers consider advice giving—often unsolicited—to be one of their main paternal duties. In fact, I think as a kid I kind of craved advice from my father. Anyway, in my senior year of high school—a time for advice seeking if ever there was one—as I pored over college catalogues and tried to imagine my future on a campus, my dad told me something that has stuck with me.

What he said was that if he ever ended up going to jail for a long time, he knew he would be okay because he had gone to college. Does that even count as advice? Of course, I was a teenager and a part of me wanted to make fun of him for saying that, probably because it was easier than trying to figure out what it meant. And dismiss it, as I imagined most teens got the chance to do with their parents every single day. But I didn't do either. Instead, I stored his comment away to interpret later.

That was over twenty years ago, and I think I've got it figured out. I think what my father meant was that in college he learned what solace and hope and joy there are in books and creative activity. That the demands they sometimes make on you are rewarding. That the stories we tell each other are vital to our nourishment.

My father doesn't give advice, but I do, compulsively. And I live in the digital age, much more than my octogenarian dad. If I ever end up going to jail for a long time, I would hope I'd be allowed to watch badly filmed YouTube rants sometimes. But I would also ask my father to send me packages filled with books—including some blank ones—knowing that when I cracked their covers, there'd be all sorts of comfort and entertainment and pleasure inside.

Sincerely yours,
Mara Faye Lethem

Mara Faye Lethem is from the outer boroughs of New York City. She enjoys both vegetables and meat. She has seen shooting stars, but that was a long time ago.

Dear Young Friend,

When I was nine years old, I learned to fly—without flapping my arms, jumping from a tree or using an airplane.

I was sitting in our living room reading an adventure story when suddenly I began to rise off the sofa and fly into ... well, into the story itself. I was no longer in our living room, reading a book. I had flown into the middle of the scene described by the words on the page.

Startled, I looked around to figure out what was going on, and instantly found myself back on the sofa. I soon learned that if I wanted to fly for more than a moment, I had to stay focused on the book. As long as I did not get distracted, I could fly into another world—the one I was reading about—leaving behind the world of family, friends, neighborhood, and school.

I'm sure that a scientist who studies the eye-brain connection could explain why it felt like I was flying. Perhaps I was so focused I fell into a trance that made me feel like my body was being transported—a trance that was broken when I lost my focus.

Science can give us facts and explanations, and that's important. But science doesn't always tell the whole truth. Even now, seventy years after my first experience of flying into a story, reading helps me fly, and will as long as I keep my imagination alive.

These days when I read it doesn't feel like my body is going anywhere—and how I miss that feeling! But a good story, a good poem, or a good set of ideas can take me to another world in my mind and heart.

There I find gifts of many sorts—comfort, challenge, excitement, insight, inspiration, vision—that I can bring back to the world to help me become a better person, and maybe help the world become a better place.

Want to learn to fly? Find a good book, stay focused on it for a while, and soon enough your mind and heart will take wing!

Yours,
Parker

Parker Palmer is a Quaker elder, educator, activist, and founder of the Center for Courage & Renewal. His books include *Healing the Heart of Democracy*; *A Hidden Wholeness*; *Let Your Life Speak*; and *On the Brink of Everything*.

Dear Readers,

Here's why I read:
I got to travel the rainy dark streets
    of London,
The sultry bayous, the exploding
    cosmos
I banished demons
I felt unexpected things for pigs
And spiders
I stopped being lonely
I met myself everywhere
I got lost
I got found
I became other people
I tried on accents and costumes
I tasted new foods
I held my breath with a brave girl in
    an attic
I developed the skills of a detective
I fell into a sea of rhythms
I stood up to monsters and tyrants
    and dangers lurking behind closed
    doors
I found a way to love the dark
I melted into the green language of
    earth
I came to believe in witches and
    spirits
I discovered that other people didn't
    feel safe or sure either
I lived their triumphs and I got
    braver
I got to be Scout Finch, Pecola
    Breedlove, Johnnie Gunther, Joan
    of Arc,

Jo March, Celie, Maya, Harriet
    Jacobs and a Prince hanging from
    a star
I fell in love
I ran away
I hopped trains, danced in taverns,
    and let down my hair
I made friends with a turtle in
    The Plaza
I learned magic
I fought battles
I felt smart
Life slowed down
I went in
I remembered
I shut out the sounds of my angry
    violent father
I took revenge sometimes with
    swords
Sometimes with fire
I flew over tall buildings
I dressed like a boy
I refused to get married
I wore amour
I slayed with poetry
I fell down a hole and got smaller
I clicked my heels on a yellow brick
    road
I rubbed a rabbit til it was real
I made new families
I refuted the mean voices in my head
I found my own

Eve Ensler

Eve Ensler is a Tony Award-winning playwright, performer, activist, and author of *The Vagina Monologues*. Her experience performing *The Vagina Monologues* inspired her to create V-Day, a global activist movement to stop violence against women and girls. She has devoted her life to stopping violence, envisioning a planet on which women and girls will be free to thrive, rather than merely survive.

Dear Young Friend,

As a little hellion, I refused to let my family read me bedtime stories like *Goodnight Moon.*

I wanted books about dinosaurs, and my mom had to intervene when grandma wasn't reading them correctly. More than once, I ended up hysterically crying, "It's *protoceratops*, Grandma, *not* triceratops!!!" (In fairness, Grandma was winging it and not reading the text). The only fiction compromise I made was *No Kiss for Mother*, about Piper Paw, a cat who hates being kissed by his doting mother. Clearly, I was a handful.

Fast forward a few years later to school, and the universe paid me back tenfold. I was a runty nerd. Wedgies became a daily humiliation. Kids mocked my bug eyes, and I begged my mother for an eye transplant. No dice.

Fishes of the World, a beautiful book of 600-plus illustrated pages, is what saved me. It became my entire world. Instead of getting punched on the playground, I would sit on a curb, safely near the classroom and teacher, dreaming of becoming a marine biologist. It showed me creatures and possibilities beyond rural Long Island. This new hunger for exploration—and love of drawing—later helped me get into Princeton University, despite the fact that my SAT scores were about as appetizing as Piper Paw's mole-innard casserole.

As an adult, I've come to realize that life isn't about finding yourself. It's about *creating* yourself. Books are clay for exactly that. Crazy adventures can be found in non-fiction, and timeless truths can be discovered in fiction. Like an artist, you blend them, and out comes a unique beauty: you.

People in Silicon Valley—where I live—like to say that you're the average of the five people you associate with most. I believe you're also the average of the five books you hold closest to your heart.

The good news is that it's never too late to find your next *Fishes of the World*. You can replace books in the inner sanctum of five whenever you want, and by doing so, change your life.

What will you read next?

Sincerely yours,
Tim

Tim Ferriss is a human guinea pig and self-experimenter. He is the author of five books, including *The 4-Hour Workweek* and *Tools of Titans*. He was also an early investor in companies like Facebook, Uber, and 50+ others. His obsessions include sharks, Japanese comic books, horseback archery, and parkour. He never had a long-term plan for life, which used to worry him a lot, but following his interests—however strange—has worked out so far.

Dear Young Friend,

The written word has the magical power of transferring thoughts from one person's brain into another's—over distance and time. I first came to appreciate this power growing up in the middle of cornfields, before the Internet. As a teenager, I realized, through books, I could access the brains of the smartest people in the world. Even people who were dead. I could tap into years of learning with the investment of just a few hours. This felt like a super power. It still does.

I've spent most of my career building systems designed to get thoughts out of people's heads and into the heads of others (hopefully, where they're useful and welcome)—because the ideas and stories we consume affect us on multiple levels and have a profound impact on how we live. The written word is the most deceptively simple tool, because it lets you impact the thoughts of others— through time and distance. Use your words.

Yours,
Ev

Ev Williams was made in Nebraska and lives in California. He is the CEO of Medium, the co-founder of Twitter, and a father of two. He likes ideas, friends, and good soup.

Dear Young Reader,

As a child, I lived in stories as much as I lived in the world. I read continuously, indiscriminately, going through nine library books in two days and then going to check out more. My mother bought stacks of novels at garage sales and thrift stores to feed my habit. Some were brittle or moldy and some were dull tales of good Christian girls or diligent wartime nurses, and I devoured them all. My favorite books I read to pieces, the pages coming off in my hands.

Now that I'm older, that feeling of sinking into a book is rarer—it's harder, because I've read so much, to find something that feels alive and new—and the more elusive that experience becomes the more I long for it. When I look back over all the time I used to spend writing about books on the Internet, I realize that mostly I wanted to find other readers who understood that yearning and could point me to new stories I'd love as much as ones I'd loved in the past.

When you love the same book as someone else, it's like sharing a secret without saying a word.

All good wishes,
Maud Newton

Maud Newton has written personal essays, cultural and literary criticism, and fiction. Her work has appeared in *Harper's Magazine, The New York Times Magazine, The Paris Review Daily, and more.* She grew up in Miami, where she was often mistaken for a tourist because of her Scottish shut-in complexion. Now she lives in Queens.

126

127

PETER BROWN

Dear Reader,

Our inventions are extensions of our bodies and our brains.

Tools like screwdrivers, pliers, and hammers are extensions of our hands. They allow us to do things that our naked hands are not hard or strong enough to do.

Running shoes, bicycles, and vehicles are extensions of our legs.

Glasses, microscopes, and telescopes are extensions of our eyes.

Cameras, voice recorders, and computers are extensions of our memories.

And the printed word is an extension of language—of our ability to get inside the minds of other people by speaking and listening to them.

Even without print, language is a powerful tool for expanding our minds. Other people can tell us what they have seen or learned, so we don't have to go through those experiences for ourselves. They can teach us how to do and make things. They can make promises and offers, so we can cooperate with them. We can divide the labor in something we want to do together: one person can offer to bring food to a party, the other the drinks.

But with reading and writing, language becomes billions of times more powerful. We can learn from people who live on the other side of the city, or the country, or the world. We can learn from people who are dead, and we can teach people who have not yet been born. We can build and do things with people we have never met face to face. There are billions of people we can learn from and work with, not just the few hundred we know in our everyday lives.

Reading also allows us to get inside the heads of people who are very different from us. A boy can appreciate a bit of what it's like to be a girl, and vice-versa. An American can learn what it's like to be an Arab, or an African, and vice-versa. An old person can learn what it's like to be a young person of today; a young person can predict what it will be like when he or she is older.

That's why, of all human inventions, it's the printed word that multiplies our powers the most.

Yours,
Steve

Steven Pinker is Johnstone Professor of Psychology at Harvard University, and the author of several books about language, mind, and human nature. His love of language became the love of his life: he met his wife thanks to an irregular verb.

Dear Reader,

Don't let anyone tell you reading makes you antisocial. That's what my grandmother said when I was young. I was an extreme case, bringing books with me everywhere—to dinner, on a sleepover—and she thought I should play more with the other kids. What she didn't get was that reading *was* play. I made some of my best friends in books: Holden Caulfield, Billy Pilgrim, Stuart Little, Harriet the Spy. They meant (still mean) everything to me, taught me that there were people who felt and thought as I did … and even more important, that there were people who would never think and feel as I did, that the world was big enough for all.

You see, my grandmother was wrong: Reading is not antisocial but the most social act we can imagine, inviting us to see, hear, feel, taste, smell someone else's life from the inside. We get so close that we become those characters, and when we emerge, we've been transformed. I wasn't antisocial: I liked to play baseball, to hang out with friends, to talk on the phone. But without reading, all that felt incomplete. My life was smaller without stories, which seemed to stream up off the pages, filling my senses like a kind of magic smoke. Magic, yes… the magic of reading, a magic so simple it's easy to overlook. Reading made me social; can we say that? Reading taught me everything I know about the world.

David L. Ulin

David L. Ulin is a 2015 Guggenheim Fellow and the author or editor of many books, including *The Lost Art of Reading: Why Books Matter in a Distracted Time*, and *Sidewalking: Coming to Terms with Los Angeles*.

Dear Reader,

Imagine all the reading you do without even realizing it—signs and billboards in the street, advertisements on the sides of buses and inside the subway, newspaper headlines and magazine covers at newsstands, banners and pop-ups online. These are unsolicited "stories" forced upon you by those who see your attention as a commodity. But you have the power to fashion your own universe through the books and stories you willingly choose to read. Books, unlike these snippets of headlines and slogans, have beginnings, middles and ends—like life itself. They reflect and explore the whole of who we are, not just the fragments selected for sensation.

Like anything worthwhile, this deeper, richer reading takes practice—it becomes both easier and more rewarding the more you do it. It's a special activity, a secret place you can visit—even if only for thirty minutes each day—and you are guaranteed to return transformed, expanded, having learned something new about the world or about yourself.

Hard and overwhelming though it may be, given all the options for what to do with your time, try to make reading a priority. Literature will thrill you, nurture your imagination, and solace you through hard times. It is an essential form of befriending yourself for life.

Yours,
Natascha

Natascha McElhone is an English-Irish stage, screen, and television actor. She has appeared in *Ronin; The Truman Show; Solaris; The Devil's Own;* and *Californication.* She is also the author of the memoir *After You: Letters of Love and Loss, to a Husband and Father,* written in the wake of her husband's sudden death in 2008. She lives in London and is the mother of three boys.

Dear Reader,

There are readers and there are Readers. If you fall into the latter category you are likely to find yourself finished reading the morning newspaper and then pulling over the cereal box to carry you through the rest of breakfast. You definitely carry a book or magazine on your way to appointments and for public transportation. You probably walk to school with a book in hand, oblivious to sidewalk impediments. The "20 minutes a day" reading assignment in grade school is unfathomable, not because it is too much time, rather because it is far too little. You might dislike overnight camp because you don't really care to make lanyards or go canoeing and would rather be reading. All of this is good. Really. Better than good—we Readers are not reading because it was assigned. We are reading because we love words, and stories, and adventure, and love, and previously unimaginable places be they real or made up.

Writing this letter turned out to be a challenge. Being a Reader doesn't automatically make you a Writer, although it makes for better odds. Some people can do both, and that is admirable. But all those Writers share one thing, they need us, the Readers.

Lise Solomon

Long in the publishing world, **Lise Solomon** still can't believe that she gets paid to read books and go to bookstores to talk about them with all kinds of wonderful booksellers.

POST NO BILLS
POST NO BILLS
KEYS MADE WHILE YOU WAIT
TEDDY
PIGGY SMALLS
PIGGY SMALLS
Z.OHORA

Dear Reader,

Greetings from United Airlines flight 107, a 9-hour flight from Munich to Newark, where I will spend several hours before boarding yet another flight, this time for Los Angeles, which I currently call home. Total travel time—22 hours. Perhaps this all sounds like a drag, a recipe for boredom and backache, but in truth I've been looking forward to taking my assigned seat so I can finally open the book I've been carrying for just this purpose: *Midnight in Europe*, a thriller by Alan Furst.

When I was eight years old, I devoured the novels of Enid Blyton, who wrote of secret societies of child detectives, who solved robberies and lesser mysteries, while rubbing shoulders with smugglers, tramps and thieves. The young detectives do not fall in love, but they always break for supper and picnics consisting of ham sandwiches, sponge cake, custard, ginger beer and more, all lovingly detailed. I remember my school librarian frowned on these little novels, and asked me to write a book report but with specific instructions: "You may read anything for this assignment, *except* Enid Blyton."

Never mind, I could still read on my own time, and I persisted with more Blyton: *The Famous Five*, *The Secret Seven*, *Noddy Goes to Toyland*, *The Naughtiest Girl in the School*, and *The Faraway Tree*—a series about three children who discover a towering tree whose upper reaches lead to alternate worlds, sometimes wondrous (with ice cream and cake), but at other times distinctly unpleasant. I suppose there is an obvious name for this kind of literature—escapist. As I grew older I put aside *The Secret Seven* and moved on, to *The Chronicles of Narnia*, *A Wizard of Earthsea*, *The Hobbit*, *The Big Sleep*, *The Black Dahlia*, *The Talented Mr. Ripley*, *Operation Shylock* and *Bring Up the Bodies*.

And so I am grateful that any time I am somewhere I don't want to be, I can open a book, climb a tree, and find myself somewhere else.

Dean Wareham

Dean Wareham is a musician and writer. Born in Wellington, New Zealand, he moved to New York City as a teenager and graduated from Harvard University. He was a founding member of the bands Galaxie 500 and Luna, and his memoir, *Black Postcards*, was published by Penguin Press.

Dear Books,

Hi, it's me. The girl who didn't like reading when she was young. Remember? I'd look at you, with all your pages, and I'd get all intimidated. Or I'd keep reading the same paragraph over and over again because I felt like the words just wouldn't go into my brain. And do you remember how I decided that reading books was for other people? How I decided that reading—like really reading, getting lost in books, finishing one book and rushing to pick up the next one, being *a reader*—was for smart people?

That was a long time ago.

After all these years, I want to write you this letter—to say thank you. Thank you, books, for waiting for me.

Thank you, after all these years, for letting me experience your exquisite and unique way of connecting me to people and places and thoughts and worlds and ideas.

Thank you for making me laugh, for making me cry, for making me feel the deep ache of hope for a hero and the deep turmoil of loathing for a villain. Thank you for making me feel deeply.

Thank you for making me think.

Thank you for giving me the gift of your stories, your wisdom and your secrets.

But most of all, thank you for your patience. You were always on my shelves, on my night tables, everywhere in the places I lived. But I never found my way *in*.

Now I have, and I'm so grateful.

I can't wait to read you all, and experience all that you have in store for me.

With much love,
Mariska

Mariska Hargitay is an Emmy Award-winning actress famous for her role as Olivia Benson on *Law & Order: Special Victims Unit*. After receiving thousands of letters from sexual assault, domestic violence, and child abuse survivors, she founded the Joyful Heart Foundation to advocate for policy change in the service of justice for survivors and to provide resources that empower them to heal.

Dear Reader,

For me, everything started with books. When growing up in Switzerland, I discovered the great writer Robert Walser and read every single word he'd ever written. Walser was my school, my inspiration to go on walks. His work gave me immense courage and without him I would never have become a curator.

Today, I want to tell you about Etel Adnan (born 1925 in Beirut), who shows us how many dimensions a book can have. The very first book of hers I saw was a long Japanese folding leporello, in which handwritten poems and signs were combined with drawings. (She was also a painter and made tapestries inspired by Oriental rugs.) I was magnetically attracted by its energy; I wanted to know more. The next day, I started to read *Sitt Marie Rose* (1977), her masterpiece and the great novel of the Lebanese Civil War. The day after that, I read her extraordinary *The Arab Apocalypse* (1989), which addresses the turmoil of war in the Arabic world beyond Lebanon and made Adnan one of the world's most important political writers, as well as a key protagonist of the peace movement. This was the first time since my early school days that I'd felt the urgent need to read the complete works of a writer. I ordered dozens of her other books, and became increasingly aware of the many dimensions of her writing: reportage, fiction, plays, her seminal *Journey to Mount Tamalpais* (1986), which explores links between nature and art, and her outstanding poetry collections such as *Sea and Fog* (2012) or *Seasons* (2008), where natural and meteorological phenomena are presented as things that imperceptibly influence and transform our skins and our souls.

Reading Adnan is addictive. As the legendary Palestinian poet Mahmoud Darwisch once said, she has never written a bad line. She's one of the greatest artists of our time, an inspiration to many people, and one of the wisest I've ever met.

It is urgent you read Etel Adnan.

All best regards
Hans Ulrich

Born in Switzerland, **Hans Ulrich Obrist** is a curator and co-director at Serpentine Galleries, London. He has curated more than 250 shows since 1991. He is the author of *The Interview Project*, an ongoing collection of interviews with artists and other creatives. So far, over 2,000 hours of interviews have been recorded.

Dear Young Hero,

Imagine you can choose your own superpower from one of these three: flying, invisibility, or being able to read. You'd be the only person in the world with that superpower. Which one do you choose? Flying is not so useful without other superpowers. Invisibility is okay for being naughty or for a little fun but not good for much else. But if you were the only person who could read ... you'd be the most powerful person on Earth. You would be able to tap into all the wisdom of the smartest people who ever lived. Their knowledge would go from their heads through squiggles on paper right into your head. You would learn things from them that no ordinary mortal would ever have enough time to learn. You would be as smart as everybody in total. Not that you have to remember it all. With reading you just look it up.

Reading is a superpower that also gives you a type of teleportation; it moves you a million miles instantly. That feeling of being immersed in a different place, or even a different time period, can be so strong you may not want to leave.

When you have this superpower you can see the world from the viewpoint of someone else. This helps protect you from the mistakes and untruths of others as well as your own ignorance.

More and more of our society is centered on pictures and images, which is a beautiful thing. But some of the most important parts of life are not visible in pictures: ideas, insights, logic, reason, mathematics, intelligence. These can't be drawn, photographed, or pictured. They have to be conveyed in words, arranged in an orderly string, and can only be understood by those who have acquired the superpower of reading.

This superpower will always be with you; it will never leave you. But like all superpowers, it increases the more you use it. It works on paper and screens. As we invent new ways to read, its value and power will expand and deepen. At any time, reading beats any other superpower you can name.

Yours,
Kevin Kelly

Kevin Kelly is Senior Maverick at *Wired*. His books include *New Rules for the New Economy*; *Out of Control*; *What Technology Wants*; and a graphic novel about angels and robots called *The Silver Cord*.

Dear Reader,

I have been trying to think of all the reasons you should read, but to be honest, all I can think of is why you most certainly should not.

Don't read if you like to be bored. Books are notorious for killing long streaks of unanchored apathy. If you're going stir crazy, wandering around the house, wondering what you're good for, for goodness' sake, don't pick up a book. You'll be on a camel's back in Cairo or inside of the mind of a physicist describing the preposterous laws of the universe in no time. Better to open and close the refrigerator door over and over again.

Don't read if the prospect of finding an unnamed part of yourself suddenly named frightens you. Sometimes you're just reading along, minding your own business, and the author suddenly puts a particular combination of innocent seeming words together and the next thing you know, BAM!, you recognize a part of yourself that you didn't know existed anywhere else in the universe, in those words, and you feel this swooning sense of interconnection to other human beings. It's disorienting. It's invasive. It's humbling. Better to avoid books and carry on in isolation, feeling smugly misunderstood.

Don't read if you know everything already. Or if you are allergic to fun. Don't read if you prefer gross generalizations to illuminating nuance. Don't read if you hate people. Or animals. Or magic.

You've been warned.

Love,
Courtney E. Martin

Courtney E. Martin has two lifelong obsessions: storytelling and solutions. She is an author, as well as a weekly columnist at *On Being*, the Peabody Award-winning public radio conversation, podcast, and website, and editor emerita at Feministing.com. When she isn't working, she is out biking with her husband and collaborator, John Cary, and her daughters, Maya and Stella, or creating unselfconscious dance parties with her amazing friends.

Dear Reader,

Today my son asked me, "Where does light go when you turn off the switch?"
I looked up, thought for a second and said, "What a wonderful question!"

I had to stop and think about it. When the switch goes off, does the light
bounce off the walls or maybe go out the window?

I know that light can travel a long, long way because when I see stars, billions
and billions of miles away, it means the light must have been traveling a long
time through space to reach me. But when that starlight enters my eyes, do I
absorb it and then, am I the end of its long journey? If it takes so long for the
light to get to me, what happens if the star dies just after the light left it? When
I look in the night sky, could I be seeing stars that are no longer there anymore?

So, where does light go when you turn off the switch?

I turned to my son and said, "I am not exactly sure."

So we looked it up in a book, because this is what books do—they allow us
to feel less alone in our uncertainty as they shed their light. I encourage you to
not let the questions that move you go unanswered. Cherish your curiosity.
It is your questions that will shape you. And your books, the kind that you love,
will continuously provoke your mind and heart to grow with a deeper sense of
understanding of yourself and how we all fit into this crazy, incredible world.

As for my questions about light, I'll leave those up to you to find out ... you
just might be inspired!

Yours,
David Delgado

David Delgado is a visual strategist at NASA's Jet Propulsion Laboratory (JPL), where he creates experiences that blend art, science, and technology to communicate the wonders found at the edge of exploration. Outside of the JPL, David is also an independent artist and co-founder of the Museum of Awe.

Dear Children, a.k.a. Future of Humanity,

Every species has its unique superpowers. Fig trees can send their roots more than 200 feet deep in search of the water they need to survive in the desert. Parasitic wasps can turn cockroaches into zombies so that they become delicious safe homes for their babies. Elephants' trunks have more than 30,000 muscles allowing them to rip down trees weighing hundreds of pounds, but also pluck a ripe berry from a bush without squashing it.

What is your superpower?

You do have one. It's something that only humans can do. Not language, not using tools, not being kind to others outside our families. Many other species have those powers. But not this one.

You, dear child, can create worlds that don't exist. You can. Amazing, incredible worlds, full of vivid detail, and characters whose emotions you can actually feel. You create these worlds using the superpower that is called your imagination. You dream, you ponder, you play, and … there it is! Does it have castles? Dragons? Crazy-beautiful robots dancing on the billowing purple sands of a distant planet? Only you know.

But even more amazingly, you can conjure up that same world in someone else's mind. You know how you do that? With words. You just tell them about it. Gently, carefully, piece by piece. Until they can see it as clearly as you can.

And when two or more humans can see the same imaginary world, extraordinary things can happen. They can play with it together. They can get excited about the events that might take place in that world. They can dream of stories and inventions and almost limitless possibilities. And sometimes, they can act to make our own world more like their imaginary world.

That's how all of human history has been possible. Wheels and boats and bridges and inventions of all kinds didn't happen by accident. They happened because people dreamed about them, shared their dreams, and then worked together to make them real.

So how do you tap into the amazing worlds created by history's most imaginative humans? That's right. You read.

The words in books will do incredible things inside your head. They'll make these alternative worlds real. They are your gateway to adventures and possibilities that will turbocharge your imagination … and inspire you to create new worlds of your own.

Read on!

Yours,
Chris Anderson

Chris Anderson was born in a remote village in Pakistan in 1957, and spent his early years in India, Pakistan and Afghanistan, where his parents worked as medical missionaries. He graduated from Oxford University in 1978, with a degree in philosophy, politics, and economics. Since 2002, he has been the curator of TED—a global platform for identifying and disseminating ideas worth spreading.

Dear Fellow Reader,

I still have on my shelf the very first book I made my parents buy for me. I was eleven at the time and the book I so urgently wanted was called *Profiles in Courage: Young Readers Edition*. In January of 1961, the author, John F. Kennedy, had just been inaugurated president of the United States, and at eleven it thrilled me that a president—my president, the one for whom I had campaigned the previous summer and fall by handing out leaflets around my neighborhood—was a writer too, as I hoped one day to be. All my favorite books were biographies of figures from the long-ago past, famous folk like Paul Revere, Robert Fulton, and presidents Abraham Lincoln and Teddy Roosevelt. Now the new president had written a book with stories about the remarkable lives of *his* great heroes. I could hardly believe my luck.

Of course, your favorite books might not be anything at all like mine. One of the best things about books is that there are so many different kinds of them, books of every flavor and description corresponding to a wide array of personalities, tastes, and needs. Without first getting to know you, I could not begin to know what favorite book of mine might possibly become a favorite of yours. But what I *can* say is: if you know of a book that you feel you *must* have, tell your parents. Chances are good they will be as glad as my parents were to get you a copy. And don't forget to pack it carefully each time you move. Not many things in life can be counted as "permanent possessions." But a few things can, and our favorite books are among them.

Leonard Marcus

Leonard S. Marcus is one of the world's leading writers about children's books and the people who create them. His own books, numbering more than 20, include *Margaret Wise Brown: Awakened by the Moon* and *Dear Genius*. Leonard also curated the New York Public Library's landmark exhibition "The ABC of It: Why Children's Books Matter."

Dear Our Future,

I don't like book reports. I don't like their formality, I don't appreciate how clinically they serve as proof of reading. I owe them big time, though. If they didn't exist, I would never have tried to avoid them, and I wouldn't have the career I have now, as a songwriter and musician.

Third grade: *Charlotte's Web*. The options are write a book report, or do something else.

I write a rap song, no backing track, very little production. I am too shy to perform it live so I tape it on my brother's boom box and then my teacher Ms. Kuster plays the cassette tape while I scrunch at my desk, very proud, but very nervous, wanting to bask in the short-lived attention but unsure how to do that with my head on my desk, under my arms. At the end of the year I win the never-before and never-after (I'm assuming) issued "Best Rapper" award.

Eighth grade: *Lord of the Flies*. Again, write a book report, or something else. OF COURSE I'm going to do something else, I am committed to hating book reports. Out of all the something else's in the world, I choose to write a song again. I double down on guitar. The song that visits me is very dark, in A minor, strummed furiously. I wail (live, this time) about Piggy, Ralph, the wild, fanged hunger in us all. This will be the work I describe in my adulthood, when people interviewing me for publications ask about the first song I ever wrote.

Adulthood: I am lucky enough to write songs for my living. Sometimes I do not know how I will conjure these things I've promised. I go back to books; I read until songs start surfacing, inspired by imagery, dialogue, characters who teach me about my family. There are no songs from me without books from Grace Paley, Denis Johnson, Marilynne Robinson, George Saunders, on and on.

Happy, happy trails going wherever books take you. May they inspire you to show your love and understanding however you will.

Your friend,
Thao

Thao Nguyen is a songwriter, musician and avid book fan based in San Francisco. She can't wait to see what you make.

Dear Generation ∞,

One of my favorite things about living in the future is that there is a place for just about anything you need to express. We have blogs, comments, web series, six-second videos, 140-character pieces of writing, and articles that have no word limit because they can run forever on the pixelated treadmill of the Internet's infinite possibilities. You can find a way to say exactly what you want to say, in the way you want to say it, and witness the work of other people who've done the same.

In the midst of my excitement, I would like to shout out books. Not because I'm worried my iPhone is turning my brain to mush, but because growing up is building and swinging across a set of monkey bars of lessons on how to live, and those lessons are easier for me to catch and hold onto if I've read them in a printed object.

Being a person is tricky, but other people do it, too—all people, in fact!—and they've recorded how. Their words reach a higher-pitched buzz of resonance in my brain once I've held them in my hands, put them on a shelf, passed them every day. Or copied them down into a journal, a book of my own, 'cause seeing them in my handwriting is more effective than just filing them away in my brain.

I know it's kind of obvious to focus on the fact that a book is a tangible object. There's something sort of beautiful about the way that technology means less clutter in the physical world. But some of that clutter makes your monkey bar set extra sturdy, makes you extra-attentive, makes you ultra-alive. And the experience of it is impossible to replicate.

Tavi Gevinson

Tavi Gevinson is an actress, writer, and the editor-in-chief of *Rookie*—an online magazine for teens, which she founded at the age of fifteen.

Dear Fellow Person,

When I was very young, I believed I was an alien creature. It was clear to me that I'd been born on another planet and sent here by mistake or as some kind of cruel joke.

Feeling different from others is a common experience, of course. There's even a word for it: "alienated."

But it's one thing to feel *like* an alien and another to truly know you *are* one. You see, on the outside I looked and acted just like the humans around me. But inside was another me that was nothing like the outside me and totally different from everyone else.

The inside me was funny and weird. It had magical thoughts and visions so wild they couldn't be expressed in words. The inside me also felt things—loves, hurts, confusions—more strongly than others did. These unearthly feelings were, I knew, inappropriate and possibly illegal.

Lying in bed, I imagined what it would be like to return to my home planet. Up there, my inside self would be totally normal. It could play and laugh with all the other inside selves. We wouldn't need our outside selves at all! We'd throw them away, like the clothes you shed at the beach on a summer day.

Then I started reading books. And in books I discovered that my inside self had a name. It was called a soul. Even more amazing, it turned out that other people had souls, too.

From then on, anytime I felt lost, a stranger in the world, I would sit quietly with a book and be reminded that I wasn't the only one.

That's why books were invented: so our souls could talk to each other. Books help our inside selves meet up and become friends, so we can find our way together through life. That's why we love them so much.

William Powers

William Powers is the author of *Hamlet's BlackBerry: Building a Good Life in the Digital Age*. A former Washington journalist, he is currently a research scientist at the MIT Media Lab. He lives with his family on Cape Cod.

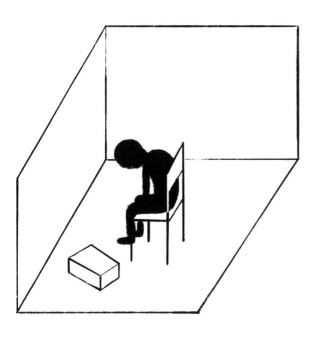
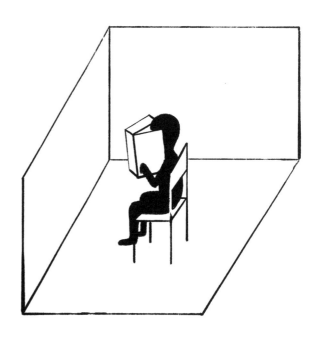
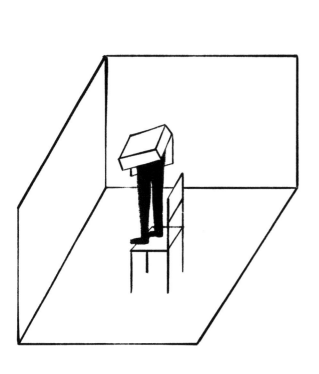
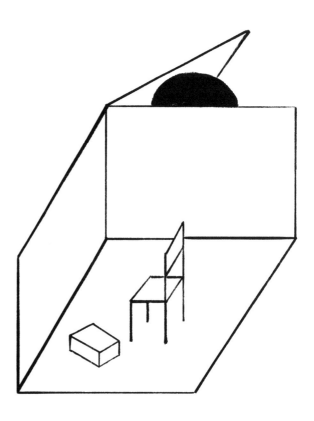

CN '15

 I LOVED THAT BOOK SO MUCH...

FROM THE DAY I FOUND IT

I COULDN'T PUT IT DOWN.

FOR WEEKS IT WENT WITH ME EVERYWHERE:

HOME, TO SCHOOL, AND THEN BACK AGAIN.

I ATE LUNCH WITH IT, HID FROM MY ENEMIES WITH IT, WENT TO BED WITH IT.

IT FELT LIKE IT'D BEEN WRITTEN JUST FOR ME...

IN FACT, IT FELT LIKE IT'D BEEN WRITTEN DIRECTLY **TO** ME...

...AND I DIDN'T WANT TO LET IT GO.

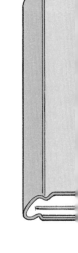

I READ IT SO MANY TIMES I ALMOST LOST COUNT.

BUT I KNEW I COULDN'T KEEP REREADING IT FOREVER.

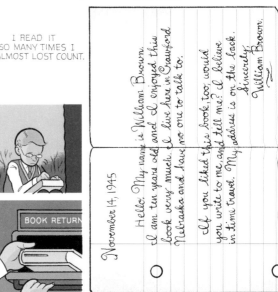

November 14, 1945

Hello. My name is William Brown. I am ten years old and I enjoyed this book very much. I live here in Crawford Nebraska and have no one to talk to.

If you liked this book, too, would you write to me, and tell me? I believe in time travel. My address is on the back.

Sincerely,
William Brown.

FOLD

BOOK RETURN

NOW, HERE'S THE *EPIC* PART:

STUCK INTO THE BACK OF THE BOOK WAS THIS FOLDED-UP PIECE OF PAPER...

AND WRITTEN ON IT WAS A LETTER FROM SOMEONE WHO'D ALSO READ THE BOOK...

ALMOST *SEVENTY YEARS AGO.*

MY MOM (SHE'S A LIBRARIAN) COULDN'T BELIEVE IT.

SHE SAID THAT I'D MADE "AN AMAZING DISCOVERY."

OF COURSE, I ALREADY KNEW THAT.

SO ONE DAY ON GOOGLE EARTH WE LOOKED UP WHERE HE LIVED...

(MOM DOESN'T "GET" STREET VIEW)

...BUT WE DIDN'T REALLY FIND MUCH, BECAUSE I GUESS GOOGLE HASN'T GOTTEN THERE YET.

A SEARCH ON HIS NAME DIDN'T WORK, EITHER...

SO I DID THE NEXT BEST THING.

I WROTE HIM BACK!

I TOLD HIM ALL ABOUT ME AND THAT IF WE WERE KIDS TOGETHER THAT HE COULD SHOW ME NEBRASKA AND I COULD SHOW HIM THE EMPIRE STATE BUILDING AND THAT WE'D BE *BEST FRIENDS FOREVER.*

OH, AND THAT I BELIEVED IN TIME TRAVEL, TOO.

To: William Brown
2 Main Street
Crawford, Nebraska
Zip Code UNKNOWN

U.S. POSTAGE
$0.49
10027
Dated Sate
04/12/2015
0689646598

I DON'T KNOW IF I'LL EVER HEAR BACK, BUT THAT'S OKAY...

IT WAS FUN TO IMAGINE.

IN THE MEANTIME, MY MOM TRIED TO FIGURE OUT HOW THE BOOK GOT HERE...

SHE THINKS MAYBE IT WAS DONATED OR SOMETHING ...BUT SINCE OUR LIBRARY THREW IT OUT (WHICH IS HOW *I* GOT IT AND WHICH SHE ALSO THINKS IS SUPER STUPID FOR LIBRARIES TO DO *ANYWAY*) WE DECIDED TO DO SOMETHING SNEAKY AND SPY-LIKE AND ACTUALLY PUT IT *BACK*...

BUT THIS TIME WITH A NOTE FROM *ME.*

AND WHO KNOWS?

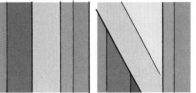

MAYBE SOMEDAY, *YOU'LL* FIND IT.

Dear Reader,

Nicolai Gogol in *The Overcoat* describes the civil servant and scribe Akaky Akakievich "who saw nothing but his own neat lines, written out in an even hand, and only if a horse muzzle, appearing from goodness knows where, came to his shoulder, and blew a gale on his cheek from its nostrils, did he become aware of the fact that he was not in the middle of a line, but rather in the middle of the street."

A library may be a safer place to read and feel protected. Gogol evokes the pleasures of being fully immersed and lost in words. How amazing that scratches on a page continue to transport us to remote places, and more importantly away from ourselves, into another world, another person's landscape. I am another. I now walk in somebody else's shoes however uncomfortable.

I am one of *The Three Musketeers*, I am *Pinocchio*, I am *The Idiot*, I am *Don Quixote*, I am *Le Misanthrope*, I am the Mad Hatter, I am *Lolita*, I am *Little Red Riding Hood and the Wolf*, I am *Huckleberry Finn*, I am *Madame Bovary*, I am *Anna Karenina*, I am *Bartleby the Scrivener*, I am Holden Caulfield, I am *Robinson Crusoe*, I am *The Hunchback of Notre-Dame*, I am Casanova. My shoes will never fit me again.

Yours,
Paul Holdengräber

Paul Holdengräber is an interviewer, curator, and writer. He is director and founder of *LIVE from the NYPL* (New York Public Library). Fluent in four languages, he has written essays and articles for journals in France, Germany, Spain, and the United States. He lives in Brooklyn with his wife and two sons.

Dear Reader,

It was seven o'clock in the evening. The book was passed out on the bottom stoop, a leaf stuck to its jacket, in front of a brownstone. It was turned over, cover side up, the way a book fans out when someone throws it down in a hurry as if reading inspired spontaneous action elsewhere. But there was no reader around. This book was abandoned. "Kwiffckft" is the sound it makes, FYI, when the crisp typeset page of a book crinkles in your fist. I know because I didn't like books. I pretend-read them. I pushed them around my shelves—mussing their pages, folding their corners, distressing their jackets—until they looked read. But I wasn't reading. I put my hand on this book. No one came. I cradled it, wondering who had left it and why. I lifted the book into my bag and took it home. The pages were thin and damp as if they had stayed in the bath too long. I myself like raisin fingers, but these pages made reading difficult. I peeled them apart. *The Adventures of Sherlock Holmes*, one said. I read each one. I placed paper towels between them as I went, reading all 202 pages this way. (202 pages equals two-and-a-half rolls of paper towel.) That was 30 years ago. After that, one by one, I took them in. Book by book, I read them all. Cared for them. Befriended their sentences. Absorbed their words. Pressed their pages. Called them by name. More years and many pages later, I love books. I love books the way I love my dog, my bicycle, and ice cream. Book by book, starting with one, I've known love that can only endure between a human and a text. And between you and me, I have never since passed a lonely book on a stoop.

Liz Danzico

Liz Danzico lives and writes in New York City with her favorite companion, a red dog. She works as a creative director for National Public Radio and also teaches people about the power of design at the School of Visual Arts.

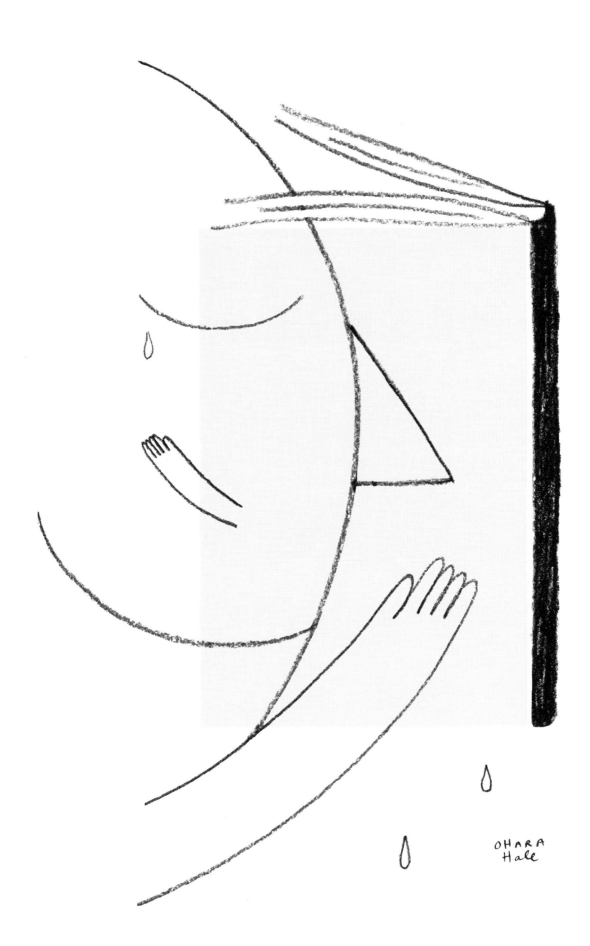

Dear Young Reader,

You can always count on a book to bring you joy. Except the badly written ones, of course, but you'll easily learn to stay away from those, like sour milk or a rotten fruit.

The good ones, the ones you will lose yourself in, will bring you immense pleasure. I said lose yourself, but maybe it's more about finding yourself. Books will give meaning and words to your experience, they will offer a name for what you sense and feel, they will make you feel connected to human beings across space and time. Books will make you laugh and cry, they will make you think and wonder, they will let you share in the universal human experience. By letting you live many lives vicariously, they will prepare you to gracefully live your own.

Be bold and playful in your reading! Fight ancient wars with the Greek heroes, travel to China with Marco Polo, climb a ladder to the Moon. Journey to the center of the Earth, watch the Big Bang happen and then wake up in a flower as a bee. Be a thief on the run from the police or a starship captain leading her crew to distant worlds. Fly across eons in the time required to read a page, or make an hour last an entire book. Feel love and hate, joy and fear, pride and remorse, suffering and rage.

You know, as a child I often read when I wasn't supposed to: during a boring lesson in school, under the bed covers when I should have been sleeping. There was a such a sense of complicity between me and the book, knowing that every read page had been a little conquest. And there was an inevitable solitude about reading, but never loneliness. In fact, if you listen carefully, as you read, you'll hear a voice whispering to you gently: "you are not alone."

Wishing you happy reading,
Samantha

Samantha Cristoforetti grew up in a small village in the Italian Alps. She gazed at the stars, read Jules Verne, and watched *Star Trek*. She dreamt of becoming an astronaut one day. On Nov 23, 2014, a Soyuz rocket took her into space. Her dream came true.

Dear Reader,

My mother once famously said, with a twinkle that made clear she thought this a charming observation—"I never knew what to do with you 'til you learned to read." Drawing a veil over the five years of my life before this moment, I have to say reading was indeed a blessing for us both. She could freely pursue her interests, and I could disappear into a life of an awaking imagination, far more interesting than my helpless efforts to amuse myself.

It started with the Sunday papers everyone seemed so interested in, scattering sections on the living room rug where I lay on my stomach, bored. I looked at the comics and could make no sense of them. "What're these squiggles in the white balloons?" said the idly curious four year old. My sister, much older, answered, "That's what those people are *saying*!" Galvanized, I learned to read in a minute, and soon graduated from funnies to comic books, *Wonder Woman* et al., and then on to whatever children's books were put in my room. I read the Marguerite Henry horse books, and Nancy Drew, of course, and fell enraptured on Tom Sawyer and Huck Finn.

I read at night, deliciously, after bedtime and "lights out." I got around this by pulling my old brown radio close to my pillow, the orange light from its glowing bulbs beaming through the vent holes in the radio's backing, casting little circles on the page. My young eyes had no problem. I docilely went to bed with a faint smile.

I became a big reader.

I still love to get into bed and read before sleep. I have a better illumination now—a slender tablet of light, with squiggles that tell "what the people are saying." About everything in the world.

Yours,
Holland Taylor

An actor and playwright, **Holland Taylor** has starred in numerous Broadway shows, films, and television series, including *The Practice; Two and a Half Men;* and *The L Word.*

Dear Young Friend,

When I was a teenager, I made a decision that changed my life. I decided that I was going to read 100 pages a day. No matter what. It was more than a decision. It was a promise to myself. Even if I felt sick, or sad, or tired, I was going to find a way to read 100 pages. No. Matter. What.

Some days it would be easy. I'd be reading a small and breezy book like *The Great Gatsby*. The pages would turn quickly, and I'd be done in less than an hour. Other days it would be very difficult. I'd be reading a big, hard-to-understand book like *The Wealth of Nations*. (I called these "vegetable books." They were hard to get through, but they made me grow.) Sometimes the books were so tough that I'd have to stay up way past my bedtime to finish all 100 pages. But I never went to sleep before I finished. No matter what.

I kept my promise for almost ten years. That's about 35,000 pages. I still read when I can: when I'm drinking coffee, when I'm on the train, when I can't fall asleep. But I'm too busy to read my 100 pages a day. And that makes me a little sad. Don't get me wrong—it's a good thing to be busy. I've gotten to do so many amazing things. I've met so many of the people that I used to only read about. I've made three books of my own. But I miss those 100 pages because they made me who I am. I'm filled up with those pages. Those pages are my thoughts and my wisdom and my dreams. Without them I'd be so much more alone. If I ever have a problem, those pages are there to help me. And I'm so happy I have them. And I'm so happy that when I was a teenager, I made a decision that changed my life.

Brandon

Brandon Stanton is the creator of *Humans of New York (HONY)*. He photographs and interviews ordinary people on the streets of New York City. Over the past several years, *HONY* has expanded to feature stories from over 20 different countries. The work is also featured in three best-selling books.

My Dear,

If you love to read, the passionate connections you make with favorite authors will be some of the realest and strongest bonds in your whole life. And some of the books you love best now are the very same ones you'll return to for comfort, wisdom and pleasure in years to come; they won't lose one iota of their old magic, but instead will become deeper and more powerful. Somehow the friendship you found in certain authors will grow with you, as if they were changing their minds along with yours over and over, as you see new possibilities in their works that you'd missed before.

I recommend that you keep the exact copy of a book that has had particular meaning for you, and write in the margins when you have an especially strong feeling. I was anciently old before I began marking my books, a practice I wish I'd begun sooner. It will recall important moments to you as keenly as a diary can.

It's especially magical how one mind can reach another clearly across centuries and cultures, breaking every barrier to connect with us. There's nothing quite like returning to a favorite author in times of trouble, or when we feel oppressed. Most of all, books liberate us from the prison of our own temporality.

So long as you have books to read and time and attention to give them, you will never be lonely, and your mind will always be free.

Affectionately,
Maria

Maria Bustillos is a journalist and critic living in Los Angeles. Her work has appeared in *Harper's*, *The New Yorker*, *The Awl*, *The New York Times*, *The Los Angeles Times*, *Tin House*, *The Guardian*, *OUT Magazine*, and many other publications.

Dear Reader,

You know how, in elementary school, your teachers always tell you to choose a "just right" book? One that you fit right into, like Goldilocks curling up in Baby Bear's chair—a book you feel comfortable in the pages of?

Those books are great. It's good to read books that feel like home.

Now, I'm not a teacher. But I am a reader and a writer, and I have another suggestion for you: sometimes, it's good to try a book that doesn't instantly feel quite so cozy and approachable. Sometimes, it's worth pushing yourself past what feels just right, and tackling a book that at first might seem uncomfortable or unfamiliar.

It could have been written fifty or a hundred years ago, when people used words differently from today. It could get off to a slower start than you're used to. The characters might seem very different from you and your friends, and behave in ways you can't imagine behaving.

But think of it as climbing up into Papa Bear's chair. Maybe it's a stretch to get up there. But maybe once you're up it's not as hard as you feared. Maybe you're bigger than you thought you were. (Remember, Baby Bear's chair broke under the weight of Goldilocks.) Yes, your feet may be dangling off the floor. But you'd never have felt those luxurious cushions against your cheek, or seen how life looks from just a bit higher up, if you hadn't tried it.

> With best wishes for your reading future,
> *Rebecca*

Rebecca Mead is a staff writer for *The New Yorker* and the author of *My Life in Middlemarch* and *One Perfect Day: The Selling of the American Wedding*. She was born in London, England, educated at Oxford University and New York University, and lives in Brooklyn.

Dear Young Friend,

I didn't grow up in a family of readers. But I always sought out books like friends across time and space. I imagined the conversations I might have with their authors—the questions I'd ask, the secrets they might tell, the kind of companions they'd be. In the life I've lived since, I've learned that there is almost always a surprising gap between the books one loves and the people who wrote them. Writers of wild stories can be homebodies, pouring all of their verve into their craft. Others produce writing that instills joy, while they themselves are crabby. Many of the best-known greats have big, messy lives.

This way books come alive, spinning free of their authors, is part of the magic. To be a reader is indeed a form of friendship all its own, sacred and mysterious. Some religious sages understand books, texts, the very letters of certain words, as living, breathing entities: words make worlds. To read is to come into kinship with ideas and images that may have been secret even to the author, until the very moment they landed on the page (or, of course, the screen). To read is to welcome this mystery of someone else's imagination into your own. To read is to take a stranger's hand and plunge into experiences you want and don't want, learning all the while to navigate the unexpected places real life will take you. To read is to experience the most humanizing of surprises: that someone else's far away mind has given rise to words with their own distinct voice and color and sound, and yet their words touch and echo and mirror places deep inside you.

The communion of reading both stretches and grounds us—word by word, white space by white space, beginning, middle, and end. And the writer's ending is, for the reader, always a beginning. What they brought into the world has entered the alchemy of your unfolding story. What you read becomes part of your human adventure, the world you will make with your words and your life.

Krista Tippett

Krista Tippett created and hosts the public radio program and podcast *On Being*. Her books include *Einstein's God* and *Becoming Wise*. In 2014, she received the National Humanities Medal.

Dear Young Reader,

The thing about books is that you can read them wherever, whenever.

On the beach, under the umbrella, slathered with sunblock, wearing a floppy hat.

Beneath the dining room table during your parents' dinner party, muffled laughter and clinking wine glasses overhead.

During long car trips, in the back seat, until you feel carsick.

Sprawled across your best friend who is immersed in her own book.

After school, instead of doing math homework.

Hidden in the corner of your great aunt and uncle's house (that smells like steamed cabbage) to avoid their wet kisses.

At the dentist's office, in the waiting room, while your dad gets his teeth cleaned.

In bed, under the covers, when you just want to finish that last chapter before your mom tells you to go to sleep.

While walking down the hallway between classes, dodging classmates until your teacher chides you for not looking where you're going.

Within the fort you build out of cushions from the couch in your living room.

Throughout the three-hour flight to North Carolina to see your cousins for the holidays, sandwiched between your grandfather, who keeps snoring, and your sister, who won't sit still.

At the library, inside a tent, on the toilet, during a thunderstorm, atop a boulder.

At least, that's what I did.

Your friend,
Emily

Emily Spivack is an artist, writer, and editor whose work draws from contemporary culture, fashion, history, and our relationship to everyday objects. She has been featured in *The New York Times*, *The Wall Street Journal*, and *The Washington Post*. She is the editor of *Worn Stories*, a *New York Times* bestselling collection of stories about clothing and memory.

Dear Reader,

If all has gone according to plan you're reading this letter in a book. It's with you wherever you are—a quiet room, a subway, or a bus. If you're reading on a bus—I truly envy you. I never mastered reading in a moving vehicle without getting carsick. Be proud of yourself.

I'm writing to you only a few days after an old bookstore I really liked closed its doors forever. Bookstores that can stay open are an endangered urban species. Everyone loves them, and wants to help, but we seem to watch helplessly from afar as they disappear.

This letter is getting depressing. I don't mean to depress you. The whole reason I brought it up was to tell you the things I loved about it, and about other book homes—shops, libraries, and even apartments.

When we emigrated from the former Soviet Union we weren't allowed to bring much—one suitcase per person. My parents shipped books, though. Poets, painters, fiction, political cartoons, music manuscripts, and vinyl records followed our path in boxes and when we moved into our tiny New York apartment they made it a home.

When you're near books, amazing things happen. They can call to you just by being in the same space as you. It can be a feeling, the color or texture of a cover, or the way it somehow sets itself apart from its neighbors and asks you to open it. Then comes the crack of the spine, the random, or not-so-random-at-all page you open to, and finally the completely surprising and unexpected words you read. In that moment, you are the only person in the world holding that book and touching its pages. You can stand there for an hour and keep reading—or put it back and start again.

That can't happen on a screen. Other wonderful things can, but not that. And moments like those—of time stopping, eyes searching and minds dreaming—are rare and important in our fast-paced lives. We must protect the possibility of them.

Good luck to us!

Your book-loving friend,
Regina

Regina Spektor is a singer-songwriter and pianist. Born in Moscow in 1980, she and her family emigrated from the Soviet Union to the Bronx when she was nine years old. Her albums include *11:11*; *Songs*; *Soviet Kitsch*; *Begin to Hope*; *Far*; *What We Saw from the Cheap Seats*; and *Remember Us to Life*.

Kids,

Reading was very important to me when I was your age. I was not interested in books that my teachers or my parents told me I should read. I wanted to discover them on my own.

I found my favorite books in the most unexpected places. On the beach or in a train station left behind by the previous owner, or in an old bookstore when the cover caught my eye and I had to have it. Reading those kinds of books was pure adventure, like taking a secret trip into an unknown land.

My advice to you: find your own special, secret book. Read it and then close your eyes and with your mind, go inside the story. With the right book, the one that is just for you, you can find a way to travel to far away places. A book like this has the power to take you in and show you the secrets and wonders of the universe.

Yours,
Marina

Since the beginning of her career in Belgrade during the early 1970s, **Marina Abramović** has pioneered performance as a visual art form. Exploring her physical and mental limits in works that ritualize the simple actions of everyday life, she has withstood pain, exhaustion, and danger in her quest for emotional and spiritual transformation.

Dear Reader,

Here is a story-letter for you...

"Ellen, what are you doing with that book? Put it away right now. We are going to visit Aunt Sadie, and you won't have any time to read. How many times have I told you it is rude to go visiting with a book?"

Mother was very strict, but Ellen hated to go anywhere without a book. It made her feel like a person without an arm or a nose. Even now that she is grown up, she can't leave her house without a book. Books make her suitcase heavy when she travels. Books lie on the floor all over her house. When you visit grown-up Ellen in Baltimore, you find books in every room. Even in the closets and the bathrooms! When Ellen was a little girl and went to other people's houses, she felt uncomfortable if she saw no books. Something was missing. Books were her friends. With a book to read, she knew she wouldn't be lonely or bored.

Once a week, Mother took Ellen and her little sister Connie to the public library. They rode on a city bus. They borrowed ten books from the Children's Room. Library Day was Ellen's favorite day of the week. She was proud of having her own library card and liked to reach up on tiptoes to give it to the librarian at the high counter who stamped all the books with their due dates. Mother said Ellen could borrow only as many books as she could carry; so you can picture the teetering tower on her lap as the bus jounced down the street on their way home.

As soon as she got inside the door, Ellen unzipped her jacket and dived into the first book like a duck. Page after page. Then, book after book. But when she got to the end of the last one, there were still many days before the next trip to the library. Mother would shake her head: "Read more slowly, Ellen."

But how could Ellen do that? It was much too exciting: there were dog stories and horse stories and pioneer stories, fairy stories, and stories about children who lived far away or long ago. At bedtime, Mother always read the girls a poem or two. The poems seemed to come from inside Mother's voice, even though she was reading them out loud from a book.

Now Ellen is a professor, and she teaches her students about books. She even writes books herself. Some of them are about children like you. At times she wonders which is nicer: reading a book or writing one for others to read. What do you think?

Yours,
Ellen Handler Spitz

Ellen Handler Spitz lives in New York with tall walls of books and a distant view of the Empire State Building. She writes, draws, teaches, and dances for pure joy. She notices strangers who remind her of characters in art, books, and opera. She recites poetry and reads aloud to children. Paris gladdens her heart, as do worlds of page, paint, clay, and song.

My Dear Reader,

I am a slow reader. I like to savor, get immersed. To not let a well-honed sentence transport me to the realms intended seems a waste of the writer's efforts and of a potential joy. So for years, I feared letting myself read too much. I worried that I would be hopelessly antisocial.

When I was young—old enough to go places by myself but not old enough to drive—I went everywhere through books. I didn't have enough money to buy all of the books I wanted. Thankfully, my pint-sized presence in bookstores "browsing" (shall we say) for hours was more amusing than alarming.

I stayed in search of an answer. What is it about writing that stretches us so? Why does reading make us feel immersed even out of doors? The accuracy to describe on the page requires far more precision than it does in conversation, where subtle gestures speak when our imperfect choices fail.

I am still a slow reader. Yet I became the person I never imagined I could become through the act of writing. To have my work read—any work at all—is merely a bonus on top of what has often been a private, life-changing event.

The dedication to revealing a truth as you see it, the courage to be a vessel for an idea pouring through: this is hidden process. You endure it. You embrace it. I know of no more direct means to become our future intended selves.

Yours,
Sarah

Sarah Lewis is an art historian, author, curator, and assistant professor at Harvard University. Her essays on race, contemporary art, and culture have appeared in *The New York Times*, *The New Yorker*, *Artforum*, various journals, and publications by the Smithsonian, The Museum of Modern Art, and Rizzoli. She served on President Obama's Arts Policy Committee.

Instructions Included.

Reach up to the shelf and pull it out
Feel the jacket, smooth and shiny
Peek under the cover, how it's bound
Smell its leaves.
Walk to a chair or sofa or a bench. Put it on your lap
Open it again and look at the pictures—read the words
Turn the page and it begins again...
The pictures. The words...
Sometimes two pages work together; sometimes there are only pictures.
Turn the page and it continues:
words, pictures, the paper and the book are
part of you, like an arm or leg
on your lap or a table
or the lap of another—the paper the pictures the words
You become part of it—your fingerprints on the paper; your sneeze
Your DNA
Your lunch. A flower you found
pressed between pages.
It holds all this for you—a good friend
in bed or in the car or plane
Open and closed.
It was once a living thing: a tree.
Bring it back to life
When you read it
—A book

Dona Ann McAdams

Dona Ann McAdams is an internationally published and exhibited photographer. She has received numerous awards for her live theater photography, as well as a Dorothea Lange-Paul Taylor Prize from Duke's Center for Documentary Studies. Her book, *Caught in the Act*, was published by Aperture, and her photographs are in the collections of the Museum of Modern Art and the Metropolitan Museum of Art.

Dear Reader,

The philosopher Bertrand Russell once said that books are read for one of two reasons: "One, that you enjoy it; the other, that you can boast about it."

Those might be our primary motives for reading, but I can think of more. A third motive is conversational enrichment. I have friends who don't read, and I value them as friends, but I also notice the frequent cul-de-sacs our conversations wander into. Resisting the urge to boast while simply changing the subject is no great burden compared to the regretful awareness of paths left untraveled. A book is a passport down those roads.

The enjoyment we get from books is hardly different from watching TV in some ways, but escaping into a book also subtly exercises parts of the mind untouched by visual media. We read for fun, and experience curious side effects. Just as our bodies have a muscle memory when riding a bicycle, our minds have "muscles" for empathy and perspective-taking that reading stretches and strengthens. The expansiveness that comes from thinking someone else's thoughts and seeing through someone else's eyes is the chief gift bestowed by the written word. That's a fourth motive: reading helps us "get" people.

At a certain point I started reading mostly non-fiction, figuring I needed to better understand the world around me. Daily life is full of truths unseen, connections unappreciated, and mysteries unexplored. A life can be lived happily and honorably within the fishbowl of its own natural perceptions, but there is nothing like reading to remove scales from the glass. An expanded awareness of how things connect, how the world is organized, and how people behave is of immense strategic value when it comes to accomplishing goals and pursuing dreams. Motive number five: reading unlocks doors.

There are lots of motives for adding new apps to your smartphone: you can play with them, you can boast about them, or you can put them to a million other uses. What apps are to smartphones, books are to brains. That's what they seem like to me anyway. What do you see in them?

Your friend in curiosity,
Baba Brinkman

Baba Brinkman is a Canadian rap artist, writer, and playwright based in New York City. He is best known for hip-hop plays and rap albums that explore the science of evolution and the stories of medieval poet Geoffrey Chaucer for a modern audience.

Ciao,

There is nothing better than a book so engrossing, you can't wait to get back (in)to it. When I was small, all books were just like that. Anything with a binding. My mom used to catch me reading the Yellow Pages with abandon. And before I could even read, I pretended to, bobbing my head ever so slightly up and down, the text evidently coming at me in waves.

There is a picture of me—actually, of my tush—taken at a children's party, except I was not really part of the party. I used to get really shy and insecure and often needed to run away and be alone. I remember that day I went into a bedroom with a book and was lying on the bed, on my tummy, a leg up, reading a book, happy as a clam. It might have even been my party. Somebody found my hideaway, opened the door, and snapped.

To this day, I read a lot. Like when I was six, twelve, twenty-five, and thirty-nine, I still need to run away. I read whenever I need to feel safe; whenever I want to feel warm or cool; whenever I need a pause; whenever I need to forget—boredom, pain, urgent tasks, anxiety; whenever I have time. I read on the subway (sometimes I even use the book as an excuse to keep my gaze low and I sneak peeks at my fellow riders' shoes), on the treadmill, in the bathroom, next to my husband Larry, by the Hudson River. I am so happy books exist.

Warmly,
Paola

Paola Antonelli's work embraces all of design, including overlooked and unforeseen applications and practices. She is the senior curator of Architecture and Design at the Museum of Modern Art in New York and the director of MoMA's new Research and Development initiative. Her goal is to insistently promote an understanding of design, until its positive impact on the world is universally acknowledged.

Dear Reader,

I have not much time to write you, and not much ink in my typewriter, but I hope I can convey a very important message before my time is up and my ink is gone.

Somewhere in the world, on some shelf or in some cupboard, in a library or a bookshop or a bedroom or a ditch, there is one book with a very important message for a specific person.

In most cases, the person has no idea which book it is, or where this book may be found, which is why most readers in the world go from book to book, from shelf to shelf, searching for the perfect read. In many cases it can take a lifetime.

People who embark on a lifetime of reading suffer many curious effects. They may have trouble paying attention in school, or during a dull dinnertime, because they are busy thinking about what is happening in a book they have been reading. They may at times confuse their friends with their favorite characters, or their enemies with their favorite villains. They may be tired in the daytime, from reading all night, or energetic in the nighttime, for the same reason. And they may find themselves looking around the world and pondering its strangeness. The strangeness of the world, like the strangeness of books, is something that is hidden from many people, at least until they start reading. Then, the strangeness is visible everywhere, and it is difficult to stop thinking about it.

But in your case, you can be spared. I have discovered the book with your specific and important message, so you can avoid a lifetime of searching. I have discovered the title and author of the book you have been looking for, or perhaps I should say the book that has been looking for you. Now that I have a little time and a little ink, I can finally inform you that

Daniel Handler is the author of several novels. As Lemony Snicket, he is responsible for numerous books for children. His books have sold more than 70 million copies and have been translated into 40 languages. He lives in San Francisco with the illustrator Lisa Brown, to whom he is married and with whom he has collaborated on several books, and one son.

A Book is a Magic Carpet

Once upon a time
When I was very small
I couldn't understand any words
    at all.

All the grown ups above my head
Knew what was up and what
    was said
But I was lost
I knew not a jot
What it was they were all going
    on about.

Then bit by bit I understood
That it was best to go to school.
If I worked hard
I'd have no regrets
Because I would learn the alphabet.

My A's and B's turned into words
Then words turned into sentences
And over time almost every line
Took me on an adventure ride.

I met tigers, piglets, bears and dogs.
I climbed magic mountains that
    I sat atop.

I explored a dark, enchanted forest.
Chartered glistening ships and stood
    with giants.
I joined secret clubs.
I flew into space.
I fought witches, wizards, warlocks
    and a dragon.
I did everything and anything
    you could ever imagine.

With a book you see you will
    never be
Bored or lonely or uninspired
And I think it's fair to say a book
Will take you anywhere you care to
    look.
A guide, a balm, a touchstone, a
    totem
Nothing can beat a good book as
    companion
Throughout this life as long as it is
You can trust in a book
A really GOOD book
To lift you up and hold your hand
And be a very best friend.

Shirley Manson

Shirley Manson is the lead singer of an alternative rock band called Garbage. She was half a century old at the time of this writing. This is her first published poem.

Dear Person/Reader/??,

People who grow up in libraries become friends. One of mine is named
Maureen. She grew up in Southern California. Her father was a doctor, her
mother a nurse. That meant they weren't home very much, and Maureen, when
she wasn't watching television, was used to bicycling aimlessly around the
suburban neighborhoods. One day, by chance, she passed a library. She was
bored rather than curious, but she went in, walked around the stacks looking
for nothing, and then randomly picked a book off a high shelf, opened it, and
read the first paragraph.

The earth sighed as it turned in its course; the shadow of night crept
gradually along the Mediterranean, and Asia was left in darkness. The
great cliff that was one day to be called Gibraltar held for a long time
a gleam of red and orange, while across from it the mountains of Atlas
showed deep blue pockets in their shining sides. The caves that surround
the Neapolitan gulf fell into a profounder shade, each giving forth from
the darkness its chiming or its booming sound. Triumph had passed from
Greece and wisdom from Egypt, but with the coming on of night they
seemed to regain their lost honors, and the land that was soon to be called
Holy prepared in the dark its wonderful burden. The sea was large enough
to hold a varied weather: a storm played about Sicily and its smoking
mountains, but at the mouth of the Nile the water lay like a wet pavement.

She thought it was the most beautiful thing she had ever read. It was the
opening—she turned to the cover—of a novel by Thornton Wilder called *The
Woman of Andros.* She biked furiously home, and that night asked her parents
if they would buy her a copy of the book. When, from behind their newspapers,
they said, Of course, dear, she knew it was hopeless. The next afternoon, she
returned to the library, got a library card, and brought the novel home. She
stayed up all night and read it by flashlight under her sheets.

The next day she went back to the Wilder shelf. Over the next few weeks she
had read all his novels. And that started her on a lifetime of reading. That one
paragraph. She eventually started teaching English literature, and ended up
becoming the Chairman of the English Department at Duke University.

That one paragraph. And it began in wonder, the delight of experiencing
words arranged into glimpses of the world that can't be found anywhere else.

J.D. McClatchy

J.D. McClatchy (1945–2018) was the author of eight books of poetry, several books of essays, and a string of
acclaimed opera libretti. He was also the editor of numerous poetry anthologies as wide ranging as LGBT love
poems and verses about birds. For the last quarter-century of his life, he taught English at Yale University, where he
also served as editor of *The Yale Review.*

THE
WOMAN
OF
ANDROS

THORNTON WILDER

Dear Kids,

Books are weapons in humankind's battle against ignorance. I don't mean like lasers and drones. I mean that knowledge is strength and the kind of knowledge you get from books is not the same as the quick fix that Googling gets you. What's more, books can't be hacked. But they can be censored, which means blocked or forbidden from being published. And this is why they are so valuable to us all. Often, in fighting ignorance, the ignorant take books prisoner. If you do not read books, then those that have been censored over the ages will be lost and forgotten. So kids, don't let them down. Read them, savor them, protect them. Don't let others make books irrelevant.

Your friend,
Steve

Steven Heller is a design writer, educator, and co-chair of the MFA Design/Designer as Author + Entrepreneur at the School of Visual Arts in New York City. He spent 33 years as art director at *The New York Times* and is the author, co-author, and/or editor of more than 100 books.

Dear Friend,

I thought I was alone in believing in the magic of human possibility, alone in the empathy I felt for the trees in the forest that get chopped down without ceremony or question as to how it will affect the birds that lived there and the wind that danced through the branches and leaves every change of season.

When I picked up two books of poems by Langston Hughes and Mary Oliver, all that changed for me. I was able to see I was not alone—not only in my feelings but in believing that everyone, including nature, has a birthright to be respected and free. I learned that what I envisioned for humanity has been envisioned many times before I was even born! This validated me in some personal way and gave me permission to keep leaning into love and justice as I grew up.

When we learn about each other, we are less afraid of each other—I am thankful to those who have come before and those who are now actively providing us maps to get to where we need to go as a human family. We are all connected and our freedom to love, learn, laugh, dream, dance is all tied up in the freedom of everyone and every living thing around us.

Love,
Morley

From Carnegie Hall to the Nomad Women's Festival in the Sahara Desert, **Morley Kamen** has brought a unique blend of jazz, folk, and soul to the world's stages. She has performed for world leaders like the Dalai Lama, Nelson Mandela, and Ban Ki-moon. Her many albums include *Sun Machine*; *Days Like These*; *Seen*; *Undivided*; and *Yoga Release (Rhythms and Improv)*.

FRANÇOISE MOULY & ART SPIEGELMAN

Dear Reader,

Absolutely amazing, this superpower of chemistry and electricity and biology you are using right now.

Somehow, through those two eyeholes in your face, you are: focusing light waves on nerve cells ... turning the light waves into electrical impulses ... sending the impulses to a squishy grey organ of about 100 billion interconnected cells in your head ... firing chemical and electrical signals between those connected cells... and recognizing the squiggle marks on this page as letters.

You are then: matching these letters with sounds in your language ... smooshing the letters into words to mean things and actions and ideas ... stringing the words together into lines called sentences ... that transfer the electro-chemical patterns I had in my squishy organ ... into the same electro-chemical patterns in your squishy organ ... through this unmatched superpower of yours called READING.

And if that isn't crazy enough, you can also use your superpower to duplicate squishy organ patterns made by other humans from all times. Patterns like:

Once upon a time... (Brothers Grimm, 206 years ago)
Sing in me, Muse, and through me tell the story. (Homer 2,768 years ago)
You're a wizard, Harry. (J.K Rowling, 21 years ago)
I am invisible ... simply because people refuse to see me. (Ralph Ellison, 66 years ago)
In nature nothing exists alone. (Rachel Carson, 56 years ago)
I rise, I rise, I rise. (Maya Angelou, 40 years ago)
To be, or not to be: that is the question. (William Shakespeare, 395 years ago)
Do you like green eggs and ham? (Dr. Seuss, 58 years ago)

Congratulations on your amazing superpower. Oh, and more good news—the more you use it, the stronger it grows. So get out there and light up as many of those electro-chemical patterns in that squishy organ of yours as you possibly can.

Really,
Jon Scieszka

Jon Scieszka is an emeritus National Ambassador for Children's Literature and the bestselling author of more than twenty-five books for kids, including *The Stinky Cheese Man and Other Fairly Stupid Tales*; *Math Curse*; *Robot Zot!*; and the *Time Warp Trio* series. Jon founded GuysRead to encourage a passion for reading among young boys, with the philosophy that boys love to read most when they are reading about things they like. A former elementary school teacher, Jon lives in Brooklyn with his family.

Dearest Reader,

I want to tell you why books are magic and how words have power.

So, there's a little girl, who lives in a house where there is a lot of anger and sadness. Maybe, she feels alone like no one understands her heart and the way it's hurting. Each day she goes to school, comes back home, and does homework. She sits with her *mami* who reads her stories of a funny maid who just can't get things right but bakes delicious pies and tarts. The little girl laughs and asks her *mami* to read it again. There it is. Did you catch it? That moment where words and books changed her life? Where a book had the power to transport her to a place where her heart did not hurt. Where she and her *mami* sit together and don't worry about anything other than sharing words and laughter. That's how sneaky books are—sometimes you don't notice how they change you, until much later.

Reader, I tell you this because it happened to me. I never understood the power that words held until 10th grade English. Ms. Agard, my teacher, loved words and wanted us to love words, too. She had us memorize the poem, "anyone lived in a pretty how town" by E.E. Cummings, a poet who often did not use capital letters, played with grammar, and even spelling; in other words, he broke the rules. Still, the poem was beautiful and I realized how much power I had; rules could be broken in writing and I could still create something beautiful. I was free to experiment with all the words because all the words belonged to me. And they belong to you, too, Reader. Words and language, just like our thoughts, have no master, no owner. Books have taught me that.

I don't know if you are like me, but if you are, you speak two languages. The problem is that, sometimes, we are taught that one language is better than another. That is lie. I remember being told that English was the only important language; even now, as an adult, I've been told that lie. Sadly, I believed that. I believed that English was the language of power. But that's not true, Reader! It's not! All your languages are powerful: Spanish, Creole, Zapotec, Lakota, Farsi, Urdu, or another kind of English (for there are many kinds of English)—are all equal. I learned this from a book, too. That book was *Chicana Falsa*, by Michele Serros. In this book, the author wrote poems and stories in English, Spanish, and even Spanglish! She wrote about *chicharrones*, taco trucks, taggers, and what it was like being a girl. She wrote about me, my culture, and my language. This book helped me see how important I am and how powerful I was. Like I said, books are magical. One minute, I was Isabel who didn't know her words mattered and the next minute I was empowered. All because of a book.

Reader, if you are reading this, you may already like books. But if you don't, give them a chance. See if they can work their magic on you and how much more powerful you become.

With Love,
Isabel Quintero

Isabel Quintero is the author of the award winning YA novel *Gabi, A Girl in Pieces*, and the chapter book *Ugly Cat and Pablo*. She is the proud taco-loving, pizza-devouring daughter of Mexican immigrants, who writes and resides in the Inland Empire of Southern California.

Dear Reader,

Books always were my best friends; ever since I was a child they shared with me their facts and knowledge, their flights of imagination, with fun, dread and suspense.

There is always a bond between the author and reader, every book is a bridge, having something different to offer—I love them, pet them on their backs, smell the ink when they are fresh out of the press, the mildew when they are old. I talk to them, as I talk to trees, stones and animals. Books are lasting, they do not lose their leaves in autumn as trees do.

I owe them my education and my fantasies. Paradise would be for me a library, to read forever and be able to remember EVERYTHING!

Yours,
Tomi Ungerer

Born in Alsace, **Tomi Ungerer** has lived and worked in New York, Canada, Ireland, and Strasbourg. An award-winning illustrator and a trilingual author, Tomi has published more than 140 books, ranging from his much-loved children's stories to his controversial adult work. Noted for his social satire and witty aphorisms, he ranges from the fantastic to the autobiographical.

man's best friend

T. Ungerer

Dear Reader,

I can hardly remember a time when I didn't want to be a reader. Even when I was, technically, a reader (insofar as I could read on my own), it was still something I wanted to be. There was always, and still is, a longing to my status as a reader—it was something I hadn't quite achieved, an aspiration, slightly out of reach. I was always—and still am—pining for the next book, though this constant state of want never spirits away enjoyment in the book currently at hand. It's just that the forward movement, the anticipation of what book comes next, is always there.

Even when everything else in my life and in my imagination fluctuated or flailed—I wanted to go into politics, no law, no advertising, no academia, no publishing—my internal drive stayed focused, underneath it all, on this one thing: I wanted to read.

Reading became my barometer, my measure, my resting point. While other children developed passions for violin or piano or soccer, I might momentarily think: Should I take horseback riding lessons? Could I learn calligraphy? My answer was almost invariably the same: I would rather spend the time reading.

For a long time, I thought of this default position as a kind of failure. Why hadn't I found my passion? What was my special talent? Did I have no offbeat skills? When it came time to write my college applications, all I had to show for myself was a diary of the titles and authors of every book I'd ever read, and a collection of my own writing. Instead of submitting one college essay, I sent in an entire packet of essays, like a folder full of excuses. I worried whether I'd manage to distinguish myself and get in anywhere.

It wasn't until later—much, much later, after I'd gotten into college and written three books, and filled pages of my "book diary" and gone into literary criticism – that I realized what I'd known all along. Wanting to read all the time, being in that state of constant aspiration, wasn't a holding pattern or an absence of desire or a lack of ambition or passion. It *was* my passion.

All those times when I'd felt apologetic about "just wanting to read my book" or about measuring the passage of time in terms of books read or ambition in terms of what I wanted to read ... It was the end goal, and a state of being. That's what readers do. When I read now, I still keep an eye out for what I'll read next. But I no longer feel like I need to make excuses for it, or feel like I should be doing something else or aspiring toward greater things. Still wanting to be a reader is enough. I wish someone had told me earlier that it's more than OK to "just" want to read. Or that I'd realized it myself.

Here's to the next book,
Pamela Paul

Pamela Paul is the editor of *The New York Times Book Review*, and also oversees books coverage for the paper. She is the author of several books, including *The Starter Marriage and the Future of Matrimony*; *Pornified*; *Parenting, Inc.*; and *My Life with Bob*. She also edited the anthology, *By the Book: Writers on Literature and the Literary Life*.

Dear Reader,

I have been thinking of Dara, a friend who got cancer while still impossibly young. At her memorial, we wore buttons emblazoned with her words: "I'm having a hard time justifying art right now." A punk rock brass band blasted grief into joy, sweaty bodies dancing wild into the night, bursting with love.

Another friend's little brother, Ted, was an artist and musician who didn't make it past his 20s. At the reception, hand-made pins that said "I ♥ Ted" were pinned onto suit jackets and silk blouses, black t-shirts and bike bags. We were an unlikely crowd, the same words written across each heart.

I liked Dara's button because it made us wonder, for a moment, together. I liked Ted's button for its simplicity. It marked us as members of the same ragged band.

Later, after Ted's reception, there was a living room and a fire. We drank wine and ate pizza and wanted to talk of other things. I asked, as I had been asking for weeks, "Why read?" John, eyes reddened with grief, sat up.

I'll tell you why reading matters, he said.

Gesturing wide, he pointed out that we are awash in information—anything you want to know, you can look it up. But you need to learn how to distinguish what is *real*. To suss out the legitimacy of a point of view. To create your own. He was talking about the difference between information and assessment, between reading and thinking. He was talking about how to be a person in the world.

Eventually, conversation turned back to our friend who had gone home grieving his little brother. We will need to love him more actively, for a bit. I bring up the difference between *sympathy* and *empathy*—something I read in a book. It turns out to be a valuable distinction. We talk about not trying to fix his grief, but just sitting with him and whatever he may be feeling. This, too, is about how to be a person in the world.

Yours,
Meehan Crist

Meehan Crist is writer-in-residence in Biological Sciences at Columbia University. Previously, she was editor-at-large at *Nautilus*, and reviews editor at *The Believer*. Her work has appeared in publications such as *The New York Times*, *The Los Angeles Times*, *The New Republic*, *The London Review of Books*, *Tin House*, *Nautilus*, *Lapham's Quarterly*, *The Believer*, *Scientific American*, and *Science*.

Dear Reader,

In their home they remembered the Sabbath day and kept it holy, which meant that from sundown on Friday until Saturday night all kinds of mundane activities were forbidden. They weren't even allowed to switch on or off any lights. There was a special device—they called it the Sabbath clock—that controlled the lights for them.

One week the Sabbath clock was broken. They ate their meal by the light of the Sabbath candles, and when those sputtered out, they climbed the dimly lit stairs to go to bed. Only that one light over the stairs had been left on.

She waited in bed a long time until she thought it was safe to creep out to the lit stairs. The library book she was burning to read was an autobiography of Louisa May Alcott, who had written her favorite novel, *Little Women*. She identified with the bookish Jo March of *Little Women* more than with any other character in any book she'd ever read. She wondered about the extent to which Jo March had actually *been* Louisa May Alcott. If there was an identity between the two, then given her own identification with Jo, it would follow that she had a kind of ghostly identity with the long-dead author.

She was so deeply immersed in her reading that she didn't hear a thing until it was too late. She jolted around and saw her mother standing above her on the top stair and sat frozen as her mother descended, a finger on her lips.

Her mother sat down beside her and silently took the book from her.

"I loved *Little Women*," her mother whispered.

Her daughter nodded, too dumbfounded to speak.

"Jo March is still one of my favorite characters," her mother continued. "What a wonderful thing it must be to create characters that live on forever."

Without another word, her mother handed the book back to her, being careful to keep her place, and climbed back up the stairs, leaving her daughter to sit in the murky light and ponder the mystery of who both she and her mother were.

Yours,
Rebecca Goldstein

Rebecca Newberger Goldstein is a professor of philosophy and also a novelist. But most of all, she is a reader who found all of her best teachers and many of her best friends in the pages of books. She liked one author's books so much that she went and married him.

Dear Young Reader,

When I was a 19-year-old undergrad, I applied for a job at a coffee shop in the West Village. I was fired two days later for "lingering too long while spreading cream cheese." Across the street, I spotted a HELP WANTED sign in the window of my favorite bookstore. Thus began my four-year employment at Un-Oppressive Non-Imperialist Bargain Books (the store's actual name).

By day I'd tackle Plato and Rousseau in the classroom; by night I'd alphabetize the Blake section of the store. After my sophomore year at NYU, I made the difficult decision to stop attending university. I was an A student and loved my classes but couldn't justify the expense ... I wanted to be a songwriter! How would I ever be able to pay off the loans?

The bookstore became my classroom; the authors, my teachers. I started with the songwriters; biographies of Bob Dylan and Woody Guthrie, prose by Patti Smith. Smith referenced Blake whom critics compared to Rumi ... I added them all to my mounting syllabus. It felt like a treasure hunt. I missed the back-and-forth of a discussion group but found so much overlap in the books themselves. These writers were all influenced by each other! Their works and ideas seemed to be having a conversation all their own.

Moving down the shelves, each section heading became an introductory course: Poetry beside Philosophy, Religion across the hall from Social Conflict. I studied R. Crumb and Rembrandt, Anime and the Impressionists. The art section was a target for neighborhood thieves and I watched over it like a hawk from my perch at the register. As time went on I took more and more pride in the small shop. When I locked up at night, the keys felt heavy in my pocket.

I didn't receive a diploma from the bookstore, but I did become a songwriter. Hidden in the spines of those books were inspirations for songs, lessons and maps for the future; all I had to do was join the conversation.

Yours,
Dawn Landes

Dawn Landes is a Kentucky-born singer-songwriter now living in Nashville, Tennessee. She has released multiple albums and her songs have been featured in commercials, films, and TV shows. Landes tours internationally and has performed with The Boston Pops, The New York City Ballet, and at TED. Her albums include *Fireproof*; *Bluebird*; and *Meet Me at the River*.

Dear Reader,

Books have been a refuge, a welcome distraction, and a source of great wisdom for me. Here are some vital life lessons I have learned:

Open and walk through most doors (there is most likely an extraordinary world beyond it).

Be kind to animals (some of them can talk).

If there is a sword in a stone try pulling it out, even if everyone says you can't.

Pick good friends. You'll need them on your journey.

Grownups don't always know everything (but before you are too delighted about that, remember: soon, you'll be a grownup too).

Trust your heart (because your brain may have been overtaken by dark forces).

Sometimes there really is a large secret society hell-bent on disrupting the world.

Listen to wise counsel, even if it comes from unlikely sources (a badger, a robot, the shy kid in school).

Pick a quest. Then embark on it. It's pretty awesome.

Rings might have powers but it's not because they're expensive or pretty.

Stand up for what you believe. Even if you have to face down bad guys. Especially if you have to face down bad guys.

Be heroic. It matters.

Yours,
Caroline Paul

Caroline Paul grew up in New England with an identical twin, a younger brother, and a menagerie of animals. She worked for a long time as a firefighter. She has written many books, including *Fighting Fire*; *East Wind, Rain*; *Lost Cat, A True story of Love, Desperation and GPS Technology*; and *The Gutsy Girl: Escapades for Your Life of Epic Adventure*.

GRANT SNIDER

Dear Young Reader,

I've found books a source of entertainment and fascination for as long as I can remember. They offer a way to learn other people's stories, to visit cultures and places you've never been, to travel back in time and forward into experiences you haven't yet had. They are an invitation to think about possibilities—imaginary worlds of the past or the future. We all have one life, but books make that life richer by letting us experience the lives of others—real or imagined.

Both fictional stories and true tales can help you learn facts and understand ideas. I avidly read fiction when I was younger, but I enjoy both fiction and nonfiction as an adult—unless I am already riveted, facts can come and go that will escape my notice. I'm grateful for the skilled author who incorporates details into a story that I can follow from beginning to end and later recall. Lists are often boring, but stories string facts together with an underlying logic that makes them both interesting and memorable. The story can be imaginary or the story can be the true one that tells how things came about or how they work.

I now do science, but I also write. I appreciate the logic that makes for a great scientific idea, as well as the art of thought that produces a great story.

You might wonder why books matter to a scientist. In terms of science itself, books taught me to explore my imagination and helped me recognize when I'd arrived at a successful conclusion. But books also introduced me to people who think like I might want to. I met people who share similar ideas or attitudes—whether scientific or not. But I also met people who think differently and invited me to do so as well.

But, ultimately, I read simply because I like to. Books make the one life we live that much richer. Life isn't always beautiful and enjoyable, but good writing always is.

Yours,
Lisa

Lisa Randall is a theoretical physicist working in particle physics and cosmology, and a professor at Harvard. Her books include *Warped Passages*; *Knocking on Heaven's Door*; and *Dark Matter and the Dinosaurs*.

Dear Young Reader,

My parents were always super busy with the family business—a little shop in Seattle that produced handmade tofu the old-fashioned way, working from pre-dawn to dusk. They both didn't go to college and weren't "book" people the way some of my friends' parents were, with their large libraries of books at their houses. But my mother had a dream that I might go to college some day, so somehow she would always set aside 20 minutes a week to take me to the library to teach me how to read increasingly harder books.

Many years later, I made it to college. And I kept accumulating more books around me each year as I got older. But those books didn't feel anything like the books I looked at in the library as a child. They were larger, but with smaller type. They were brand new, and I was the only one who would read them. I kept them on the shelf with my other books acquired each year through every class I took. Each book got me further in life, and further away from that early experience with my mom at the library. I treasure that beginning; it was figuratively the very first page of my own life book.

Nowadays, I think of how a book can contain both the dreams of the author and everyone that is supporting the author's dreams, and they can also contain the dreams of the reader who supports the author's dream. And if you can imagine all the books out there, and all the people reading those books, and all the authors, and all those people around the readers and the authors. Well, there you go. The many pages of paper bound simply together as a book are binding the lives of many people together, too.

Reading makes me think of my mother. I am bound to her, my life, through books.

Best wishes,
John Maeda

John Maeda is an artist, graphic designer, computer scientist, and educator dedicated to bringing design to technology. The former President of RISD, he became a leading voice in the STEAM movement. He is the author of many books, including *Creative Code: Aesthetics + Computation*; and *The Laws of Simplicity: Design, Technology, Business, Life.*

Dear Reader,

"Better immersion ... than to live untouched." — *Tillie Olsen*

I have been crazy for books since I was a little girl. My family moved nearly every year. I would arrive in each new place not knowing a soul. So I would head to the library. I knew there would be friends and adventures living within the bookshelves.

When I was older, I took a trip to Brazil, charting my course through the plots of Jorge Amado's novels, taking buses across Itabuna, sitting beside women with chickens on their heads. A few years later, I moved to Africa, carrying a guitar, some clothes and a box of books that allowed me to bring the whole world with me.

Books by Africa's own sons and daughters—Achebe, wa Thiong'o, Soyinka, Gordimer (the list is long)—taught me to see, to *feel* the continent's many places and peoples. Those books became my guides for interpretation, teaching me to ask the questions. To stay open. To understand that every life, every family, every city, state and nation is a composite of the beautiful, ugly, shimmering, dull, chaotic, peaceful, colorful, quiet and exquisite world that is ours.

Modern life will pull you toward so many distractions. Push them away for books, for the love of ideas, for constant friends who will share their truths, if not *the* truth. Immerse yourself in worlds created and understood by the author's own immersion.

The more books you read, the more you will pay attention. The more you will wonder and discover. The best books will become like talismans, touchstones, prayers that imprint the soul.

So read, my friend. Embrace the world. Come home to yourself.

Yours,
Jacqueline Novogratz

Jacqueline Novogratz is the founder and CEO of Acumen, a venture capital fund that serves the world's poor, who typically live on less than $4 a day. Her work creating Rwanda's first microfinance institution inspired her to write, *The Blue Sweater: Bridging the Gap Between Rich and Poor in an Interconnected World*.

Warning! Stop reading!

Don't you kids realize how dangerous books can be?

Stories can take you to far away places without permission slips from your parents. They might also keep you up way past your bedtime with a flashlight under your covers.

Knowing the tales of great heroes might help you give a rousing speech to your classmates and start an anti-homework revolution. If you dive into cookbooks, you could make your own scrumptious food and forever be free of the school cafeteria. Other books might even show you how to code software for a robot that cleans up your bedroom. Oh no!

Spending more time with books might make you smarter than your teachers. Can you imagine their embarrassment when *you* have to help *them* fix their quiz mistakes? Then they'll need you to teach the other children that "sagacity" means wisdom and a "thalweg" is the lowest point of a riverbed or valley.

Overall, can't you see how terrible this could be? If you keep reading, you might learn so much that you can take over for the adults and then you kids will be in charge! You all could be the journalists, entrepreneurs, artists, professors, authors, doctors, explorers, scientists, and even the leaders of our countries! Then what would the grown-ups do? Live in a world run by brilliant, interesting, innovative, and compassionate young people? Ugh. No, thank you.

So, please stop reading before you become really smart, successful, and happy.

Signed,
Mr. Chris Sacca
GRUMPY OLD BUSINESSMAN

Chris Sacca is a venture capital investor, company advisor, and entrepreneur. When not on the road for his companies, or huddled up in the cramped apartments and coffee shops where his entrepreneurs often write their code, Chris lives with his family in both Truckee and Los Angeles, California.

The world is alive, generous,
and waiting patiently for us
to figure it out.

This is an amazing time to be alive.
Of this I am now convinced.

~

Believe only half of what you read
and none of what you hear.

Walk instead in the company of
the wisdom of the sages and ages,
and find yourself in the harmonic rhythms
of eternity sung in their writings.

~

We know if we go.
The way books do show.
So endlessly we grow.

~

Believe only half of what you see
and none of what you read.

Books don't teach us about life,
they just call forth what
our mind suspects,
our heart hopes,
and our spirit knows
to be true.

~

The world is alive, generous
and waiting patiently for us
to figure it out.

This is an amazing time to be alive.
Of this I am now convinced.

Tom De Blasis

Tom De Blasis is a writer, photographer, painter, musician, innovator, humanitarian, gardener, designer, and artist. He is the founder of (tbd) collective, a social innovation design practice, and echolands, a restorative ecology service. He was previously design innovation director at the Nike Foundation and design director at Nike for global football and the Olympics. Tom is based in Portland and is at times all of, more than, and none of these.

Dear Reader,

Most dragons don't know how to read.
They hiss and fume and guard their hoard.
A tasty knight is what they need
For dinner (they spit out the sword),
Then go to sleep on heaps of treasure.
They've no use for the written word.
But I learned early to take pleasure
In reading tales and poetry,
And soon I knew that I preferred
Reading a book to fighting knights.
I lived on apple pie and tea,
Which a kind lady made for me,
And all my days and half my nights
Were spent in reading story-books,
A life more thrilling than it looks.
Now that I'm old and cannot see
To read, the lady's youngest child
Comes every day to read to me,
A cheerful child named Valentine.
We're both as happy as can be
Among the treasures I have piled
In heaps around my apple tree.
No other dragon watches curled
Around such riches as are mine,
My Word-hoard, my dear Library:
For every book contains a world!

    Yours truly,
    Bedraug (Smaug's Second Cousin Once Removed)

[BY URSULA K. LE GUIN]

Ursula K. Le Guin (1929–2018) was one of the greatest science fiction and fantasy writers of all time, and a formidable essayist. In her eighty-eight years, she moved the hearts and minds of generations with beloved works like *The Left Hand of Darkness*; *City of Illusions*; and the *Earthsea* series.

©C.Vess'15

My Dear Young Friends of Today and Tomorrow,

Let me tell you about three heroes of mine growing up. They were all fictional, or perhaps they existed in mythology, in distant history, but for a boy saddled with an overactive imagination, these three larger-than-life figures became very real. Strange but true—King Arthur, Robin Hood, and Sherlock Holmes are still my heroes some fifty years later. I'll tell you why.

I was born in France to Chinese parents, and we moved to the United States when I was seven. Life as a new arrival was very confusing. Everything was different. To navigate this unfamiliar culture, I needed guidance beyond what my immigrant parents could provide.

As I spent a fair amount of time alone, I turned to reading. I read and reread every version of *King Arthur and the Knights of the Round Table* I could lay my hands on. The notion that people could pursue "quests" with an almost impossible goal to find the "Holy Grail" smacked of adventure, heroism, human frailty and accidental destiny. I was hooked.

When my family landed on these shores, John Fitzgerald Kennedy was president. His administration was likened to King Arthur's Camelot. Many years later, I think of the Silk Road Ensemble—a global group of musicians I formed—as a present-day version of the Knights of the Round Table. We go on quests, we seek adventure, we try to do good, and are willing to dream the impossible dream.

There was another band that captured my adolescent imagination—Robin Hood and his Merry Men. They appealed to my sense of fairness and justice. Robin Hood was a hero to me because he was so strong and shrewd that he could live and thrive in a totally corrupt world by creating his own society in the Sherwood Forest while constantly challenging those in power. This combination of skill, smarts, and the impulse to right wrongs while having fun shaped my sense of social justice and informed my idea of citizen musicians and artists working to respond to people's needs.

Finally, there is the great detective Sherlock Holmes who solves the most complex mysteries by sheer brain power and deductive ability, fusing logical reasoning and empathetic thinking to plumb the depth of the human psyche. While he doesn't quite break the law, he realizes the law's limitations. He understands human frailty. He has great confidence in his abilities, but he never lets ego cloud his judgment. Much of my work as a musician requires the same psychological puzzle-solving to identify who a composer is and figure out what motivates him or her to create music.

In your encounters with books, may you find your own heroes who will be your lifelong companions and help you build your own creative world.

Your friend in words, thoughts, and action,
Yo-Yo

Yo-Yo Ma is a cellist and a passionate cross-pollinator of genres, cultures, and disciplines. The recipient of more than 15 Grammy Awards, he is the founder of Silkroad—a global collective of musicians and artists who create music engaging their many native traditions.

Dear Reader,

I co-own a bookstore in Nashville, Tennessee, called Parnassus Books. When my friend Karen Hayes and I opened the store in the fall of 2011, everyone told us we were crazy. *Bookstores are dead!* people would say. *Reading is dead!*

But it turned out those naysayers were wrong. Ever since we opened the doors on that first day, people have poured in wanting to talk about the books they've read and ask what they should read next. I knew from a lifetime of personal experience that people like being around books. People like the companionship books provide, the extra lives they enable us to live. Stories and books and reading are far too essential a part of being human at this point to let them go.

Still, nothing that matters in life should be taken for granted, so if you love to read, here's how you can ensure that the generation after you and the generations after them will keep at it: all you have to do is read books. Sometimes you should read them in public places. At least some of the time read books that are printed on paper and hold them up so people can see what you're doing. When they say, "Is that book any good?" stop reading for a minute and answer them. The wonder of books is that they are worlds we enter into alone, and yet at the same time they can connect us to other people.

I keep a book with me all the time, the way a hiker might keep a bottle of water and a box of matches. The book is essential to my survival. Without the book I would only be myself, but with the book there is no end to all the people I can be.

Yours most sincerely,
Ann Patchett

Ann Patchett is the author of *The Patron Saint of Liars; Taft; The Magician's Assistant; Bel Canto; Run; State of Wonder;* and *Commonwealth.* In November 2011, she opened Parnassus Books in Nashville, Tennessee, with her business partner Karen Hayes. She lives in Nashville with her husband, Karl VanDevender, and their dog, Sparky.

Dear Reader,

For as long as I can remember, my life has included books. Before I could read there were my mother's arms, my father's arms, the particular scents of my parents as I leaned back into them and listened to the words. *Pat the Bunny, Goodnight Moon, The Tale of Peter Rabbit.* As I grew older, we read *Millions of Cats, The Story of Babar.* And then *Stuart Little, The Wonderful Wizard of Oz, The Story of Doctor Dolittle.* I learned to read and discovered my mother's old books: The *Little House* series, the *Mary Poppins* books, *The Peterkin Papers.* My mother and I read together, lying on my bed like teenagers. Each week my sister and I went to the library where we could check out ten books each—an armload. I marveled at the lives to be discovered, at history come to life. *Understood Betsy, The Five Little Peppers and How They Grew, Betsy-Tacey and Tib.*

My life, my childhood, was happy. But it was just one life, lived on Dodds Lane in Princeton, New Jersey, in the middle of the twentieth century. I opened the cover of *The Secret Garden,* though, and like magic I found myself living Mary Lennox's life decades earlier in Misselthwaite Manor in Yorkshire, England. I opened the cover of *Pippi Longstocking* and found myself residing— without any adults—in an enormous house with a horse and a monkey.

I'm sixty years old now and my passion for books hasn't wavered. Letters becoming words, words becoming stories, stories becoming lives. I want to read them all and live them all.

Yours,
Ann Martin

Ann Martin is the author of many books for young readers, including *A Corner of the Universe* (a Newbery Honor book); *Rain Reign*; the Doll People books (written with Laura Godwin); and the Baby-sitters Club series. She lives in Ulster County, New York, where she's involved with animal rescue.

246

KAISA & CHRISTOFFER LEKA

Dear Reader,

You shouldn't be able to read at all. Think about it. Funny little shapes, the letters. They don't look like anything. When ancient people began writing, they started with pictures ☀☙≈ and we can still do that ☂☕✄, but the letters of the alphabet — A B C D — are symbols with no meaning. They're hard to learn, even though there is a helpful song.

If the goal is to get information about the world into your brain, a video should be much more efficient: ready-made images, no concentration required. The skill of reading is unnatural, like macramé and chess. In fact, for most of history, only a lucky few people could read and write.

Yet somehow you do learn to read. Then, when you open a book, you scarcely see the letters or even the words. They vanish, an invisible blur across the printed page, while the information they encode pours into your mind as if through a fire hose. Look. Listen. Moonlight shining in the window; a mysterious smile glimpsed in a mirror; a muffled cry from a distant room; the squelch of wet shoes on the tile. Sights and sounds rise from the page and mingle with your experience and stir your memories. You fill in the empty spaces. There is no reading without imagination.

Opening a book is opening a door: you step through; you forget where you are. Time passes, but not for you. You walk into a dream—someone else's dream, but it becomes your own. You remember a food you've never tasted, a song you've never heard. Homesickness comes over you—a sorrowful longing for a place that was never your home. Or you fall in love with someone who never existed. How can that happen? Information is entering your brain by way of your eyes, yes, but it feels as though something has reached straight through your ribcage and grabbed your heart.

Yours,
James Gleick

James Gleick thinks and writes about science, history, and how ideas connect. His books have explored chaos theory, time travel, the life of information, and the life of Isaac Newton. Even though he writes nonfiction, he reads mostly novels and stories. Sometimes he plays tournament bridge for fun. He lives in New York City with his wife Cynthia Crossen and a soft black dog named Jazz.

Dear Friend,

Books won't make you a better person. Some of the worst people in the world have loved books. Books will teach you stuff, but so will YouTube videos and science documentaries. What books alone can give you is the feeling that the book is reading you. Books provide the one kind of time travel that works, where you make a wish and actually become a musketeer in Paris or a used-car salesman in Pennsylvania. The miracle of a book is that it is just black marks on a white surface, and they make worlds. Or, rather, they are the only thing that lets you make worlds and go places that look just the way you want them to look.

Someone else will try to tell you that the best books are the ones that take you farthest and show you most. "The great thing about literature is that you soon learn that the best writing, expressing the deepest ideas, is the most transporting." Memorize this lie; it is incredibly useful. But don't think it's true. I've been transported by very bad books just as far away and as surely as by good ones.

So: read with terrible posture. Read whatever you happen to pick up. Read bad books that hold your attention, and you will find it easier to read good ones that take a bit more work before the leap elsewhere takes place. Read only for pleasure, and you will find that you read for life.

AG

A staff writer for *The New Yorker* since 1986, **Adam Gopnik** was born in Philadelphia and raised in Montreal. He received his BA in Art History from McGill University before completing his graduate work at the Institute of Fine Arts, New York University. He lives in New York City with his wife, filmmaker Martha Parker, and their two children, Luke Auden and Olivia Esme Claire.

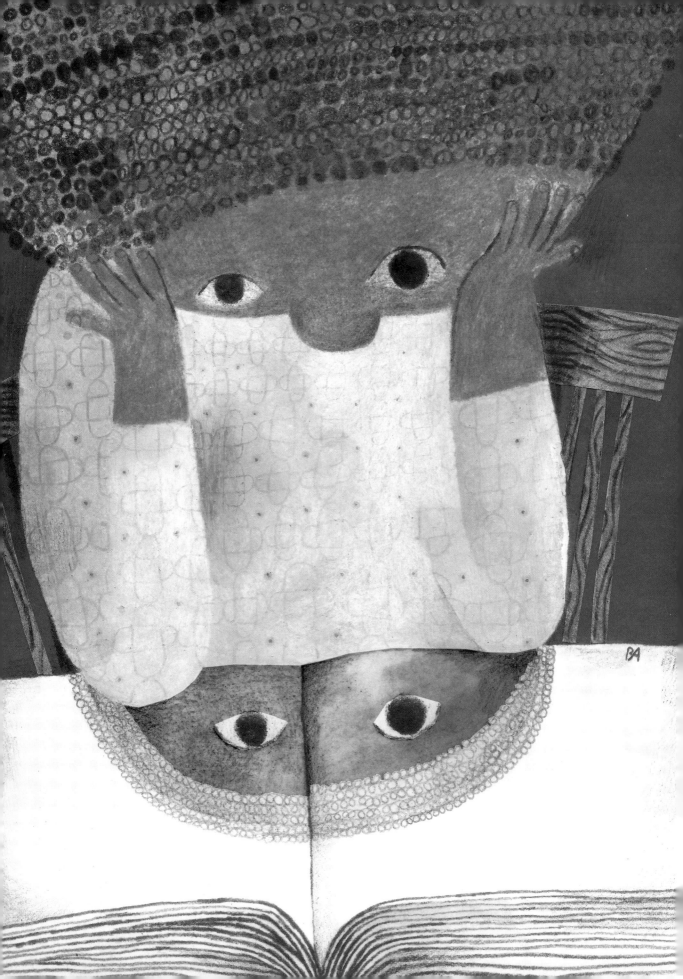

Dear Reader,

I don't remember my childhood books well. But there are still some stories I've always known: "I've known for as long as I can remember," is the saying. I do remember reading to my son, Gibson, how silent he became, this rambunctious, willful boy. He'd settle into the crook of my arm, proving evolution designed that specific shape in my body just for that purpose. I'd cradle him while we both faced the hard pages of the book, the hard colorful pages of the book that I don't remember from my own childhood. He'd soften and settle instantly as though hypnotized, reassuringly heavy, transfixed on the page, quiet in anticipation of the words warm in his hair.

My mother taught me to read. I don't mean that she taught me to sound out the syllables, although she may have done that too. I mean she taught me how to read. The book that stands out in my memory at the cusp of my exit from my childhood is *Beloved*. She saw layers in *Beloved*, detected meanings I missed, projected some of herself onto characters. So I read the book again to see more of what she saw. I could hear her voice on the second reading, slowing the book to a different pace. Sometimes I hear such rhythm in the phrasing of prose that I've tried to borrow melodies, steal them outright.

I've tried to write about math with the energy of *Cannery Row*. I've tried to write about a colossal scientific machine with the tenderness of *The Human Stain*. I never borrow words, not intentionally at least, but I borrow rhythms.

My son's first words were a rhythmic conglomerate: "Warethwiillletheensarrrr." He'd start strong but still rise to a roar, "WIIIIILLLLLE," bringing the song back down to the quieter growl, "arrrrrrr." As he practiced the notes, the expression sharpened but only slightly, barely enough to resolve in our minds. He focused on me, joyous just mystified by my lack of comprehension: "WarethWIIIILLLLEtheensarrrr," he said motionless, staring, imploring me to finally understand. We howled as I repeated triumphant and he repeated and I repeated:

"*Where the Wild Things Are!*"

I can't predict which books Gibson will remember. A prodigious musician in his preteens, he only reads biographies—about Jimi Hendrix and Robert Johnson, Howlin' Wolf, and Janis Joplin. But his ear for music (inherited from his father) so wildly exceeds mine that now he teaches me how to listen to songs, understand layers that I missed, and sometimes I can hear what he hears.

Books look static and quiet but they are not. They exude a pressure. They have a melody and stride. But they are only effective when balanced by the pressure of the reader, when they can reflect as well as transmit, when they elongate or quicken according to the velocity of the reader. You, reader, define the experience of the book. Every book you read could only be read in precisely that way by you.

Yours,
Janna

Janna Levin is an astrophysicist, a professor of physics and astronomy at Barnard College, the author of *How the Universe Got Its Spots*; *A Madman Dreams of Turing Machines*; and *Black Hole Blues*. She is also the Director of Sciences at Pioneer Works—a cultural center for cross-disciplinary experimentation in Brooklyn.

Hi You,

I really want you to hear what I am going to say, because I think it is the truth. Okay? I'll make it fast.

If you love to read, or learn to love reading, you will have an amazing life. Period. Life will always have hardships, pressure, and incredibly annoying people, but books will make it all worthwhile. In books, you will find your North Star, and you will find you, which is why you are here.

Books are paper ships, to all the worlds, to ancient Egypt, outer space, eternity, into the childhood of your favorite musician, and—the most precious stunning journey of all—into your own heart, your own family, your own history and future and body.

Out of these flat almost two-dimensional boxes of paper will spring mountains, lions, concerts, galaxies, heroes. You will meet people who have been all but destroyed, who have risen up and will bring you with them. Books and stories are medicine, plaster casts for broken lives and hearts, slings for weakened spirits. And in reading, you will laugh harder than you ever imagined laughing, and this will be magic, heaven, and salvation. I promise.

Okay? Deal?

Love you,
Anne Lamott

Anne Lamott is *The New York Times* bestselling author of *Help, Thanks, Wow*; *Small Victories*; *Stitches*; *Some Assembly Required*; *Grace (Eventually)*; *Plan B*; *Traveling Mercies*; *Bird by Bird*; *Operating Instructions*; *Hallelujah Anyway*; *Imperfect Birds*; *Rosie*; and more. A recipient of a Guggenheim Fellowship and an inductee into the California Hall of Fame, she lives in Northern California.

Dears,

My grandmother Wenonah Bond Logan was the most beloved friend of my childhood. She grew up in the racially segregated US South in the early part of the twentieth century, mostly in Alabama. Her family moved to Washington, DC, when she was a teenager; the nation's capital was also then the segregated South.

Long before she was my grandmother she was a girl with two long, thick braids who used to roller skate to the embassies a few miles from her home and sit on the steps "to imagine the rest of the world was there," as she'd one day tell me. She'd then continued to stoke her imagining of elsewhere, skating to the public library on Mount Vernon Place to take out stacks of books. She liked to read about other places so she could imagine them, she told me. Most of her friends stayed forever in Washington—nothing wrong with that. But my grandmother's reading made her dream. Her girlfriends gathered at the train station and wept as they waved her off to storied points north and the hopes of further education, more books.

In the 1920s she wrote to a university in Denmark: *I am what is known as an American Negro, and I imagine you have never known one. Will you invite me to come and study at your school?* This was one of my favorite of her stories. Why Denmark, I would ask her, entranced by her tales of smorgasbord, the puzzle ring she brought back from a suitor that one day became mine, and the sari she began to wear after being mistaken for Indian. *Because when I was a teenager I read about the statue of the little mermaid being built, in Copenhagen harbor, and I wanted to see it for myself.*

My grandmother's much older sister Carrie was given the privilege of choosing her baby sister's name. She chose Wenonah because she had read it in a book, in Longfellow's poem "Hiawatha." In that poem—which I most remember with the phrase, "On the banks of the Gitchee Goomee"—was found the name for the treasured baby sister who would grow to read books, imagine worlds far beyond her own, and then go out to find them. The unusual beauty of that most apt name was only to be found in the pages of a book.

Love,
Elizabeth Alexander

Elizabeth Alexander is a poet, essayist, professor at Columbia University, and President of the Andrew H. Mellon Foundation. She is the author of several collections of poems and essays, a play, and the memoir *The Light of the World*. In 2009, she became the fourth poet in history to read at a U.S. Presidential inauguration, where she welcomed Barack Obama to the presidency with her poem "Praise Song for the Day," composed for the occasion.

Artists

16 **Lara Hawthorne** currently lives and works in the vibrant city of Bristol, UK. She is the author and illustrator of *Herberto*, which has been published in Portugal, Brazil, Slovenia, France, and South Korea. Lara has also illustrated Poet Laureate Carol Ann Duffy's 2016 Christmas poem, *The King of Christmas*, published by Picador.

18 **Ping Zhu** is a freelance illustrator who has worked with clients big and small, won some awards based on the work she did for the aforementioned clients, attracted new clients with shiny awards, and who hopes to maintain her livelihood in Brooklyn by repeating that cycle.

20 **Frank Viva** is an illustrator and designer. His first book for children, *Along a Long Road*, was a *New York Times* Best Illustrated Book. He is also the author of *A Long Way Away*, which received multiple starred reviews, and *Outstanding in the Rain*. Viva runs Viva & Co., an award-winning branding and design agency in Toronto.

22 **Sophie Blackall** is the illustrator of over 30 books for children, including *Finding Winnie*, which won the Caldecott Medal in 2016. Her series *Ivy and Bean* is a *New York Times* best seller. She has also done commissions for the MTA and MoMA, and global campaigns for UNICEF.

24 **Mouni Feddag** is an illustrator and shelf-stacker born and based in Nottingham, UK. Her name is Algerian and her humor is British, but she studied graphic design and spent most of her life in Frankfurt, Germany. She has drawn for *Real Simple*, Anthropologie, and *Vogue* online.

26 **Olivier Tallec** graduated from the Ecole Supérieure d'Arts Graphiques in Paris and worked as a graphic designer before devoting himself to illustration. Over the past 25 years he has done hundreds of editorial illustrations as well as picture books and cartoons for children and adults.

28 **Christian Robinson** is a picture book illustrator and animator based in San Francisco. His *Last Stop on Market Street*, written by Matt de la Peña, was both a 2016 Caldecott and Coretta Scott King honor book. It also won the 2016 Newbery Medal. Moreover, Robinson has worked with the Sesame Street Workshop and Pixar Animation Studios.

30 **Daniel Salmieri** grew up drawing ninja turtles, fighter jets, and 90s Knicks players. He has since gone on to create illustrations for award-winning children's books and *The New York Times*. Dan lives with his wife Sophia and their dog Ronni in Brooklyn, New York, where he was born and raised.

32 **JooHee Yoon** is an illustrator and printmaker who regularly contributes to publications such as *The New York Times* and *The New Yorker*. She also has published several picture books, one of which was selected as a *New York Times* Best Illustrated Book. She has taught illustration and printmaking at RISD, along with leading workshops abroad.

34 **Michela Buttignol** is a New York-based Italian designer whose technological ability has enabled her to work in a variety of mediums. She holds a BFA in illustration from IED Milano and also undertook an intensive studies program in graphic design at Parsons, The New School. Her work has been recognized and awarded by the Society of Illustrators, *American Illustration* and *Creative Quarterly*.

36 **Liniers**, born in Argentina in 1973, began making fanzines for his friends when he realized law school was not for him. Since 2002, his daily comic *Macanudo* has appeared in *La Nación*, Argentina's largest newspaper. He has published more than thirty books. With his wife Angie, he also founded Editorial Común to publish graphic novels by local and foreign authors. He and Angie now live in Vermont with their three daughters.

38 **Marianne Dubuc** has published several books that have been translated into more than 20 languages. Her book *The Lion and the Bird* was the recipient of the 2014 Governor General's Award in Illustration, and her book *The Coach* won the 2015 TD Children's Literature Prize. She lives in Montreal where she divides her time between her pencils and her family—her greatest happiness!

40 **Felicita Sala** was born in Rome in 1981. She is a self-taught illustrator who grew up in Perth and graduated with a degree in Philosophy from the University of Western Australia. She has worked on several stop-motion animations and occasionally makes editorial illustrations, but her passion is illustrating picture books. She lives in Rome with her husband and their daughter Nina.

42 **Ashleigh Corrin** is a graphic designer by day, illustrator by night, who lives in Virginia with her husband. Her artistic talent comes from her late grandmother who inspired her to serve people's unique stories with creativity. With her illustrations, Ashleigh hopes to contribute good laughs, nostalgia, vulnerability, transparency, and the opportunity to see the light in ourselves and others.

44 **Taeeun Yoo** received her MFA from the School of Visual Arts. Her first picture book, *The Little Red Fish*, was awarded the Society of Illustrators' 2007 Founders Award. A two-time recipient of the *New York Times* Best Illustrated Book Award, she has also illustrated the reissues of Madeleine L'Engle's renowned series *The Time Quintet* and *The Austin Chronicles*. Taeeun lives in South Korea.

46 **Øyvind Torseter** is a Norwegian artist and illustrator. He has made many books of his own and several together with different authors. Torseter has received numerous prizes for his books, including the Bologna Ragazzi Award, the Norwegian Book Art Prize, and the Nordic Council Children´s Literature Prize. His books have been translated into over 20 languages.

48 **Cindy Derby** is an artist based in San Francisco. She is the author and illustrator of the upcoming picture book *How to Walk an Ant*. Her background is in puppetry and she has traveled all over the world with her puppets.

50 **Yara Kono** made her first drawings on the wall of the living room. Her mother was not too pleased at first, but finally gave in to the "artistic talents" of her daughter. From wall to paper, from paper to computer, the years have gone by. Since 2004, Yara has been part of the Planeta Tangerina team.

52 **Kristin Roskifte** is a Norwegian illustrator and picture book author. She has written and illustrated seven picture books. Some have won awards and been translated into several languages. Roskifte has also worked on a range of different illustration projects. She loves sketchbooks, coffee, and long runs.

54 **Violeta López** is an Ibicencan born in 1980. She has made illustrations for picture books, magazines, animations, apps, interiors, television shows, and apparel. Her interests lie more in learning through a process than in creating a product. She is very glad to be published for the first time in the US by Enchanted Lion.

56 **Esme Shapiro** is an award-winning illustrator and author of books for children. She wrote and illustrated her debut book, *Ooko*, in 2016 and has since illustrated *Yak and Dove* by Kyo Maclear. A graduate of the Rhode Island School of Design, she has exhibited at the Society of Illustrators and her work has been featured in *Taproot* and *Plansponsor* magazines.

58 **Ingrid Godon** was born in 1958 in Wilrijk, Belgium. After 20 years of drawing for others, she decided it was time to make her own book. The result—*Hello, Sailor*—won international acclaim and has been translated into French, German, English, and Korean. Ingrid still draws for her inner child and is glad her images continue to move the hearts of children.

60 **Dasha Tolstikova**, originally from Moscow, now lives in Brooklyn, New York, with her dog Muffin. Her books have received lots of stars and have been translated into many languages.

62 **Matthew Forsythe** lives in Montreal, where he makes books and comics.

64 **Mandana Sadat** was born in Brussels, lived in Tehran until the age of four, then moved with her family to Paris, where she still lives. She treasures the cheerfulness and openness she felt as a child when moving from one culture to another. She has devoted herself to children's book illustration since graduating from the Strasbourg École supérieure des arts décoratifs in 1997.

66 **Josh Cochran** grew up in Taiwan and California. He specializes in bright, dense, conceptual drawings. His work spans a variety of media including large-scale mural installations and children's books. Currently, he lives in Brooklyn, New York. He loves a good taco and the cold side of a pillow.

68 **Carson Ellis** creates art for The Decemberists and is the author and illustrator of the bestselling picture books *Du Iz Tak?* and *Home*. She lives on a farm in Oregon with her husband and two kids.

70 **Roz Chast** is a longtime cartoonist for *The New Yorker*. Her books include *Can't We Talk About Something More Pleasant?* and *Going into Town: A Love Letter to New York*.

72 **Maisie Paradise Shearring** was born in Hull, UK. She studied illustration at Edinburgh College of Art and recieved her MA in Children's Book Illustration at the Cambridge School of Art. In 2015, Maisie was awarded the International Illustrators Award at the Bologna Children's Book Fair. She recently completed her first book as both author and illustrator: *Anna and Otis*.

74 **Chloe Bonfield** is an illustrator/author of children's books. She divides her time between the city and the countryside. Chloe is fascinated by the relationship between culture and nature, and the wonder of the everyday. She looks for magic and enchantment in the places in-between, and in the spots where all of these things entwine with technology.

76 **Guillermo Decurgez** (**Decur**) was born in Rosario, Argentina, in 1981. He is a cartoonist and the author/illustrator of such books as *Merci!; Semillas 1; Pipí Cucú*; and *Mi Cajón Favorito*. He is also a contributing illustrator to the Argentinian newspaper *La Nación*. He has exhibited his paintings in France, Spain, Chile, Bolivia, Columbia, La Rioja, Buenos Aires, and Rosario. He is a lover of old roll-top desks, rare beings, and nature.

78 **Valerio Vidali**, born in Lodi in 1983, is an Italian illustrator and designer based in Berlin. He has won the Ilustrarte Prize (Portugal) and the CJ Picture Book Award (South Korea). Valerio's work has also been selected several times for the Bologna Illustrators Exhibition, and he has been published in more than a dozen countries.

80 **You Jung Byun** is an award-winning illustrator, storyteller, and lecturer. Her debut book *Dream Friends* was published in 2013 to critical acclaim. Her client list includes *The New York Times*, Penguin Books, Nobrow Press, NPR, Verizon, Rodale, J. Walter Thompson, Gestalten, the Society of Children's Book Writers and Illustrators, and more.

82   **Ariana Fields** is a graduate of the SFAI printmaking program and received her Masters in Landscape Architecture from City College. She is interested in visual modes of storytelling and has a passion for working on paper—everything from drawing and printmaking to mapping and design.

84   **Christopher Silas Neal** is an award-winning illustrator and author who regularly contributes to *The New York Times* and *The New Yorker;* he also creates book covers for various publishers. He has directed short animated videos for Kate Spade and Anthropologie, and was awarded a medal from the Society of Illustrators for his work in motion graphics.

86   **Lisa D'Andrea** lives and works in Padua, Italy. She spent her childhood in Friuli, northern Italy. She attended the International School of Comics of Padua, and since graduating has been devoted to drawing and painting as an self-taught artist.

88   **Katrin Stangl**, born in 1977, studied at the Leipzig Academy of Visual Arts. She is an illustrator of words, both her own and other people's, and uses a variety of techniques, including woodcut, silkscreen, drawing, and lithography. She has received multiple awards for her graphic reproductions and illustrations. She lives with her family in Cologne, Germany.

90   **Ariel Schrag** is the author of the novel *Adam* and the graphic memoirs *Awkward; Definition; Potential*; and *Likewise*. Her writing and comics have appeared in publications such as *New York Magazine, Cosmopolitan*, and *Medium*. She has been a television series writer for HBO and Showtime.

92   **Marc Johns** is an artist who makes drawings that are sometimes funny, and sometimes not. He lives in Victoria, British Columbia, with his wife, two sons, and a jar full of pens.

94   **Hyewon Yum** is the author and illustrator of *Puddle; The Twins' Blankets; The Twins' Little Sister; Last Night* (a Fiction Honorable Mention for the Bologna Ragazzi Award and winner of the Golden Kite Award); and *Mom, It's My First Day of Kindergarten!*, which won the Ezra Jack Keats New Illustrator Award. She lives in Brooklyn, New York.

96   **Wendy MacNaughton** is a *New York Times* best-selling illustrator and graphic journalist based in San Francisco.

98   **Albertine** is an artist and illustrator. She has frequent exhibitions in Geneva, Lausanne, Morges, Paris, and Rome. Her collaboration with Germano Zullo has led to many publications, and their books have been translated internationally. Albertine is also an editorial, poster, and advertising illustrator. She has taught printmaking and illustration for over 17 years at the High School of Art & Design in Geneva, Switzerland.

100   **Catarina Sobral** was born in Portugal in 1985 and is a published author and illustrator. After studying graphic design, she graduated with a degree in illustration in 2012. Her illustrations are a regular presence in editorials and on album covers and posters. She has had ten books published in eleven different languages.

102   **William Grill** is a London-based illustrator who has worked for clients like *The New York Times*, Amnesty International, Harrods, and *Shelter*. His books include *Shackleton's Journey*, which won the 2015 Kate Greenaway Award and has been translated into over 14 languages, and *The Wolves of Currumpaw*.

104   **Anne Slaughter** is an artist living in Charlottesville, Virginia. Her work includes landscapes, collages, and mixed media exploring the physical and emotional traces of the passage of time in nature and in our human endeavors. She has had over 20 one-woman shows nationally and internationally.

106 **Cecilia Ruiz** is a Mexican author, illustrator, and graphic designer based in Brooklyn, New York. She debuted as an author in 2015 with *The Book of Memory Gaps*. Her most recent book is *A Gift from Abuela*. Cecilia's work has appeared in *The New York Times*, *Fast Company*, *Hemispheres*, *Life & Style*, and more.

108 **Nahid Kazemi** is an Iranian artist who has published children's books in Iran and other countries. She holds a BA and MA in visual art and painting from the Art University of Tehran, and has participated in professional festivals and exhibitions around the world. She lives in Montreal and is working on several books with Enchanted Lion.

110 **Jenni Desmond** lives in London and is the author and illustrator of several picture books, including *The Polar Bear*, which was a *New York Times* Best Illustrated Book of 2016. Her work is admired for its narrative and visual depth, being at once complex and simple.

112 **Tallulah Fontaine** is a freelance illustrator and artist originally from Edmonton, Alberta. She currently splits her time between Toronto and Los Angeles, where she makes watercolors and drawings.

114 **Sophie Gilmore** works with watercolor and the finest little pens to illustrate the curious and untrue, and occasionally a little humor finds its way in, too. She lives on a boat in London, and likely daydreams too much.

116 **Emily Hughes** is an Asian-American illustrator based in London, UK, who was influenced by her upbringing outdoors on the big island of Hawaii. She has worked on picture books with Flying Eye, Walker, and Chronicle Books.

118 **Mo Willems**' work in children's books, animation, television, and theater has garnered him three Caldecott Honors, two Geisel Medals, six Emmy Awards, five Geisel Honors, and a Helen Hayes nomination. He is best known for his characters Knuffle Bunny, The Pigeon, and Elephant and Piggie.

120 **Tim Miller** is the author and illustrator of *Moo Moo in a Tutu*. He is also the illustrator of *Snappsy the Alligator (Did Not Ask to Be in This Book)*; *Margarash*; and the middle-grade series *Hamstersaurus Rex*. Tim studied at the School of Visual Arts in New York. He currently lives in Jersey City.

122 **Kenard Pak** illustrates picture books and book covers. Experience working at big animation companies may have given his art a cinematic feel. His main inspiration, however, comes from memories and mundane observations. Originally from Maryland, Kenard now lives in San Francisco.

124 **Ofra Amit** is an illustrator who lives and works in Tel Aviv. She loves illustrating books, through which she explores the symbiotic relationship between text and image. Her work has earned her several awards, including the 3x3 Gold Medal, the Society of Illustrators Gold and Silver Medals, the IBBY Honor Award, and the Israel Museum Award.

126 **Hadley Hooper** lives in Denver and works as an illustrator and painter. She is the groundskeeper, gallery coordinator, and co-owner of Ironton Studios. She is also a co-founder and board member of the River North Art District, RiNo for short. She lives in an old house in a now-trendy neighborhood with Hugh Graham and Maddie the dog.

128 **Zoey Abbott** lives in Portland, Oregon, with her husband and kids. Her first two books are *Twindergarten* by Nikki Ehrlich and *Finn's Feather* by Rachel Noble. Zoey loves telling stories and making things with her hands.

130 **Benjamin Chaud** was born in the Alps in 1975 and studied drawing in Paris and Strasbourg. He has illustrated more than 70 books, including the *Pomelo* series, and is author-illustrator of *The Bear's Song* and *Farewell Floppy*. Honors include a gold medal from the Society of Illustrators and selection for the jury of the Illustrators Annual at the 2015 Bologna Children's Book Fair.

132 **Brian Floca** is the author/illustrator of numerous books for children, including *Locomotive* (2014 Caldecott Medal) and *Moonshot: The Flight of Apollo 11*. Floca's books have been selected twice for the *New York Times* Best Illustrated Children's Book list. He was born and raised in Temple, Texas, and now lives and works in Brooklyn, New York.

134 **Peter Brown** lives in Brooklyn, New York, where he writes and illustrates books for children. His picture books include *The Curious Garden; Children Make Terrible Pets; Creepy Carrots!*; and *Mr. Tiger Goes Wild*. His first novel for children is entitled *The Wild Robot*.

136 **Marine Rivoal** is a French author and illustrator. She loves acid-etching and printmaking and continues to develop her artistic techniques on a number of editorial projects. In 2016 she finished production of *Iâhmès and the Great Devourer*, co-directed with Claire Sichez, which was preselected for Best Animated Short Film at the 2017 César Awards.

138 **Gemma Correll** is a cartoonist, writer, illustrator, and all-around small person. She is the author of *A Cat's Life*; *A Pug's Guide to Etiquette*; and *The Worrier's Guide to Life*, among other books. She publishes her "Four Eyes" cartoon at GoComics and at The Nib on Medium. Her illustration clients include Hallmark, *The New York Times*, Oxford University Press, Knock Knock, Chronicle Books, and *The Observer*.

140 **Bernardo P. Carvalho** was born in 1973 in Lisbon, where he attended the College of Fine Arts. He won the second CJ Picture Book Award in South Korea and has been honored by the Leipzig Book Fair for best book design. He is a co-founder of Planeta Tangerina.

142 **Zachariah OHora** is the illustrator of the *New York Times* bestseller *Wolfie the Bunny*. His *The Not So Quiet Library* was named one of the *Boston Globe*'s Best Books of 2016. His latest book is *Niblet & Ralph*. He lives and works in Narberth, Pennsylvania.

144 **Benoît Delhomme** was born in 1961 in Paris. An acclaimed cinematographer, he has shot more than 35 movies, including *The Scent of Green Papaya* and *The Theory of Everything*. He has also painted and drawn for 20 years and had his first solo show in New York in March 2017 at the Daniel Cooney Fine Art Gallery.

146 **Samantha Cotterill** is the illustrator of several books for children, including *Charlotte and the Rock* and *The Forever Garden*. She is also the author-illustrator of *No More Bows*. Samantha lives and works from her home in Upstate New York with her husband and two boys.

148 **Serge Bloch** is an illustrator and author of children's books but mainly works as an editorial illustrator. He enjoys doing humorous work, calling it "work of modest art." He has won two Gold Medals from the Society of Illustrators and the Bologna Ragazzi Award, among others.

150 **Andrea Tsurumi** is an illustrator and cartoonist who lives in Philadelphia and who deeply loves libraries. Her books include *Why Would You Do That?* and *Accident!*

152 **Isol**, born in 1972 in Buenos Aires, is an illustrator and author. With 22 titles published in 17 languages, her specialty is narration using images and words. In 2013, she was honored with the Astrid Lindgren Memorial Award (ALMA), one of the most prestigious distinctions in children's literature.

154 The **Brothers Hilts** are Ben (the older one) and Sean (the younger one). They work as a team illustrating, designing, and constantly comparing to see whose ideas are better. They are also the products of an insomniac family and a long line of people who stay up late into the night. Sean went to Rhode Island School of Design and Ben went to Cooper Union in New York City. They now live and work in Cambridge, Massachusetts.

156 **Brian Rea** produces drawings and paintings for magazines, murals, fashion, and film projects. His work has been exhibited in Paris, New York, Seoul, Los Angeles, and Barcelona. An Adjunct Associate Professor at Art Center College of Design and a member of Alliance Graphique Internationale, he lives in Los Angeles with his wife, his son, and his plants.

158 **Julia Rothman** works in Brooklyn, New York. She graduated from RISD in 2002. Some of her clients include Chronicle Books, Target, Anthropologie, Crate & Barrel, *The New York Times*, *The Washington Post*, Urban Outfitters, The Metropolitan Transit Authority, *Food and Wine*, and Victoria's Secret. Besides working, Julia enjoys going on walks with her terrier Rudy and playing Boggle on her iPhone.

160 **Sean G. Qualls** is an award-winning children's book illustrator, author, and artist. His books include *Grandad Mandela*; *Emmanuel's Dream*, which won an ALA Schneider Award, and *The Case for Loving* and *Two Friends*, both of which were co-illustrated with his wife, Selina Alko. He lives in Brooklyn (where you can find him DJing on occasion) with his wife and their two children.

162 **Vittoria Facchini** was born in the south of Italy and studied editorial graphic design in Florence. She began her career illustrating for Italian wine producers, and later worked for organizations dealing with immigration, rare genetic disorders, autism, and disability. In 1997, she started making picture books that focus on gender diversity and sexuality. She creates mixed-media installations and leads workshops for children and adults.

164 **Christoph Niemann** is an illustrator and author. He has created covers for *The New Yorker* and *The New York Times Magazine*. His books include *Sunday Sketching* and *WORDS*, a visual dictionary of the 300 most common English words.

166 **Chris Ware** is a cartoonist and graphic novelist. He is the author of *Jimmy Corrigan: The Smartest Kid on Earth* as well as *Building Stories* and *Soot City*, among others. He is a frequent contributor to *The New Yorker*.

168 **Maira Kalman** was born in Tel Aviv and moved to New York with her family at the age of four. She was raised in the bucolic Riverdale neighborhood of the Bronx. She now lives in Manhattan.

170 **Ohara Hale** is a Montreal-based multidisciplinary artist. She sings, writes, draws, dances, and performs questions and ideas about love, life, and anything and everything else in between, unseen, unknown, and dreamed. Her most recent book is *Be Still, Life*.

172 **John Parra** is an illustrator, teacher, and fine artist. His children's books have earned recognition including SCBWI's Golden Kite and a Pura Belpré Honor. In 2015, John was invited by the Metropolitan Museum of Art to present a special event about his work. In 2017, his art appeared on six new Forever Postage Stamps. John lives with his wife Maria in Queens, New York.

174 **Oliver Jeffers**'s award-winning work takes many forms, from figurative painting to installation, illustration and picture-book making. His picture books—including the *New York Times* bestseller *The Day the Crayons Quit* and its sequel, *The Day the Crayons Came Home*—have been translated into over 30 languages. Oliver is from Belfast, Northern Ireland, and now lives and works in Brooklyn, New York.

176 **Sara Varon** is a printmaker, graphic novelist, and children's book author/illustrator living in Brooklyn. Her books include *Odd Duck*; *Bake Sale*; *Robot Dreams*; and *Chicken & Cat*. Sara was a recipient of the 2013 Maurice Sendak Fellowship. She currently teaches at the School of Visual Arts in New York.

178 **Sergio Ruzzier** is an author and illustrator of picture books. Born in Milan, Italy, in 1966, he has been living in Brooklyn, New York, since 1995. He was a recipient of the 2011 Sendak Fellowship. His most recent picture books are *This Is Not a Picture Book!* and *Two Mice*.

180 Illustrator **Sonia Sánchez** paints with both traditional and digital brushes, using layers of texture to evoke emotion and movement. Her debut picture book *Here I Am!* received two starred reviews and was nominated for the prestigious Eisner Award in the category of Best Painter/Multimedia Artist (Interior). She lives with her husband and a sleepyhead cat in a blue house near the Mediterranean Sea.

182 **Judith Clay** was born and raised in northern Bavaria, Germany, where she completed an apprenticeship in ceramic painting and later earned a degree in comparative literature. She now works as an independent artist. She has written and illustrated a children's book, has had artwork published in magazines and textbooks, and has exhibited all around Europe.

184 **Liz Starin** is an illustrator, writer, software developer, and former children's book reviewer living in Brooklyn. Some of her books include *Roar!*, written by Tammi Sauer, *Splashdance*, and *Captain Monty Takes the Plunge*, written by Jennifer Mook-Sang.

186 **Benji Davies** is an award-winning author and illustrator of children's books, notably *The Storm Whale* and *Grandad's Island*. In his work, he strives to capture the sights, sounds, and feelings of childhood—as he remembers it. He lives and works in London.

188 **Lia Halloran** is an artist who flies small planes on Earth and dreams of flying in space. She lives in Los Angeles with her wife, two dogs, a 40-year-old desert tortoise, and a cat named Holden Caulfield.

190 **Sandra Jávera** is an illustrator and designer living in Brooklyn, New York. Trained in São Paulo, she graduated in 2011 with a degree in architecture. She creates illustrations for magazines and newspapers, and patterns for textiles and wallpaper. She has illustrated over 10 books, including a new edition of the classic *The Little Prince*. Sandra also enjoys working with ceramics.

192 **Julie Paschkis** was born in 1957 and grew up in Pennsylvania. She attended Germantown Friends School, Ringerike Folkehogskole in Norway, Cornell University, and the School for American Craftsmen at RIT. She taught art to children for several years, and has been painting and illustrating full time since 1991. She lives in Seattle with her husband Joe Max Emminger, a painter.

194 **Marc Drumwright** left his home in Houston, Texas, to study art, design, and creative writing at the Kansas City Art Institute. While in school, he worked at an independent bookstore named The Reading Reptile. Marc came to New York to attend the Columbia Publishing Course and to work as Jon Scieszka's assistant. He currently lives in Brooklyn and works at Enchanted Lion Books.

196 **Lizi Boyd** has written and illustrated many children's books. Her titles include *Inside Outside*; *Flashlight*; *Big Bear Little Chair*; *I Wrote You a Note*; and *A Name for Baby*.

198 **Kris Di Giacomo**, an American living in France since age 12, has always felt like a bit of an odd fish. Childhood is the culture she relates to most, and drawing was her first language, which makes illustrating children's books her ideal job. Over the years, she has worked with different authors and publishers to illustrate over 40 books, many of which have been translated worldwide.

200 **Lisa Brown** is an illustrator, author and cartoonist. Her books include *The Airport Book* and *Goldfish Ghost* (with author Lemony Snicket). She is currently at work on a graphic novel about a carnival sideshow, but can mostly be found wasting time online.

202 **RUMISU** is the joint project of two sisters, Pinar and Deniz. Born and raised in Istanbul, Turkey, Deniz Yegen Ikiiski studied fashion design at Pratt while Pinar Yegen studied economics at Harvard, and then finance at Wharton Business School. RUMISU is built on their mutual love of illustration, design, handmade elements and ethical production and consumption.

204 **Chip Kidd** is a graphic designer and writer based in New York City. He was married to the writer J.D. McClatchy.

206 **Pascal Blanchet** is an illustrator and graphic artist from Quebec, Canada.

208 **Miguel Pang Ly** is an illustrator born in Barcelona of Cambodian and Chinese parents. His main interest is to explore the depths of a story and the unconscious. His clients include SM, Abuenpaso, Windsor & Newton, Blind Books, and Mov Palavras. His work has won many awards and has been selected for the Illustrators Exhibition at the Bologna Children's Book Fair.

210 **Françoise Mouly** joined *The New Yorker* as art editor in 1993 and has been responsible for over 1,000 covers, many of which were chosen by The American Society of Magazine Editors as Best Cover of the Year. She is the publisher and editorial director of TOON Books, which publishes comics and visual narratives for young readers.

210 **Art Spiegelman** almost single-handedly brought comic books out of the toy closet and onto literature shelves. In 1992, he won the Pulitzer Prize for his masterful Holocaust narrative *Maus*, which portrayed Jews as mice and Nazis as cats. His comics are best known for their shifting graphic styles, formal complexity, and controversial content.

212 **Henrik Drescher** was born in Copenhagen in 1955 and his family emigrated to the United States in 1967. He studied for one semester at the School of the Museum of Fine Arts in Boston in 1974, after which he began working in illustration around Boston.

214 **Sabina Hahn** is a freelance illustrator, animator, and sculptor currently based in Brooklyn, New York. She is also a co-founder of Interval Studios.

216 **Tomi Ungerer** was born in Alsace and has lived and worked in New York, Canada, Ireland, and Strasbourg. An award-winning illustrator and a trilingual author, Tomi has published more than 140 books, ranging from his much-loved children's stories to his controversial adult work. Noted for his social satire and witty aphorisms, his work ranges from the fantastic to the autobiographical.

218 **Alessandro Sanna** was born in 1975 and lives in Mantua, Italy. He teaches illustration at the Academy of Fine Arts in Bologna. An author and illustrator of picture books, he was a finalist for the 2016 Hans Christian Andersen Award.

220 **Jon Klassen** is an author/illustrator, mostly of picture books, and many of those about hats. He lives and works in Los Angeles and is originally from Ontario, Canada.

222 **Giselle Potter** has illustrated over thirty children's books, including *The Year I Didn't Go to School*, about traveling with her parents' puppet troupe in Italy when she was eight. She also illustrates a weekly column for *The New York Times* called "Ties."

224 **Elise Hurst**, born and living in Australia, is a self-taught artist, illustrator, and writer specializing in children's books. She is particularly known for her surreal nostalgic and anthropomorphic works, full of sumptuous detail, which have made their way around the world in many forms.

226 **Grant Snider** is the creator of Incidental Comics and the author of *The Shape of Ideas*. He lives in Wichita, Kansas, with his family, where he practices cartooning and orthodontics.

228 **Luke Ramsey** co-founded the Islands Fold residency, exhibits internationally, and works in public art, painting, and freelance illustration. His client list includes *The New York Times*, Patagonia, British Columbia Children's Hospital, and more. His book *Intelligent Sentient?* was nominated for a Doug Wright Award.

230 **Katie Harnett** is an illustrator based in the UK. She is a graduate of the University of the West of England and the Cambridge School of Art. Her work was exhibited in the Illustrators Exhibition at the Bologna Children's Book Fair in 2012 and 2015, and she was the recipient of the Bologna Children's Book Fair Ars In Fabula Grant Award in 2015.

232 **Isabelle Arsenault** is the illustrator of acclaimed children's books such as *Jane, the Fox, and Me*. She has won Canada's prestigious Governor General's Literary Award three times and two of her picture books were named *New York Times* Best Illustrated Books of the Year. She lives in Montreal.

234 **Carla Torres** is an Illustrator born and raised in Quito, Ecuador. In 2005, she landed in New York City looking to expand her mind, soul, and vision as an artist. Since then, her work has been exhibited locally and internationally and has won several illustration awards.

236 **Shaun Tan** grew up in the northern suburbs of Perth, Western Australia. In school he became known as the "good drawer," which partly compensated for always being the shortest kid in every class. He graduated from the University of Washington in 1995, with joint honors in Fine Arts and English Literature. He currently works as an artist and author in Melbourne.

238 **Charles Vess**'s illustrations include Neil Gaiman's novel *Stardust* and cover art for Marvel, DC, Tor, and Subterranean Press. He has won four World Fantasy, three Chesley, a Mythopoeic and two Eisner awards. His work has been featured in many galleries, including the Museum of Comic and Cartoon Art and the Museum of American Illustration at the Society of Illustrators.

240 **Narges Mohammadi** studied Graphic Design at Shahed Art University in Tehran, and has since illustrated over twenty books. She has received international recognition for her work and has won many awards, such as the CJ Picture Book Award in South Korea. Narges has been featured in the prestigious Bologna Illustrators Exhibition several times.

242 **Vladimir Radunsky** created more than 30 children's books, which are known all over the world. His books have received numerous awards and recognitions, including selection for the *New York Times* Best Illustrated Children's Book list. Born in Russia, Vladimir lived his adult life between New York and Rome.

244 **Robin Rosenthal** is a freelance illustrator and creative director who specializes in designing and developing products for children and their parents. Formerly an art director at the award-winning *Martha Stewart Kids* magazine, Robin has gone on to design a line of modern posters for kid's rooms and Paper Town Friends, an iPhone app for kids.

246 **Kaisa** and **Christoffer Leka** are artists who publish graphic novels about their bike trips and other adventures. They live in Finland.

248 **Benoit Tardif** offers simple, colorful images. Often tinged with irony, his style is marked by an interest in silk-screen and posters. Benoit works with traditional and digital techniques to build images that are designed to convey a specific, conceptual message. He works in Montreal, where he lives with his wife and son.

250 **Beatrice Alemagna** was born in Bologna, Italy, in 1973. When she was a child her biggest heroes were Pippi Longstocking, Marcovaldo, Karlsson-on-the-Roof, Sylvester, and Meffi. At eight she decided that whatever the cost, once grown up, she would become a painter and writer of novels.

252 Brothers **Eric Fan** and **Terry Fan** received their formal art training at the Ontario College of Art and Design in Toronto. Their work is a blend of traditional and contemporary techniques, using ink or graphite mixed with digital media. *The Night Gardener* was their first picture book, followed by *Ocean Meets Sky.*

254 **Andrea Dezsö** works across a broad range of media: drawing, painting, artist's books, embroidery, installation, and large-scale public art. She has three permanent public artworks in New York City and exhibits internationally.

256 **R. Gregory Christie** is an Atlanta-based commercial artist and illustrator with over 20 years of experience and over 50 books to his name. He currently works as a freelance illustrator and owns GAS-ART Gifts, located in Decatur, Georgia. He also enjoys book binding and teaching young people about art and literacy.

EDITORS

Maria Popova is a reader and a writer, and the author of *Figuring.* She writes about what she reads on Brain Pickings (brainpickings.org), which is included in the Library of Congress permanent digital archive of culturally valuable materials. She rereads *The Little Prince* every year and discovers new wisdom, new beauty, new gladness each time.

Claudia Zoe Bedrick is the publisher, editor, and art director of Enchanted Lion Books, an award-winning, family-owned company in Greenpoint, Brooklyn. The thoughtfulness and creativity of her son, her nieces and nephews, the young people with whom she works, and of children everywhere nourish her sense of hope every single day.

DESIGNER

Jonathan Yamakami is a graphic designer who has worked with publishers in Brazil, India, and the United States. He was born in São Paulo, earned his MFA from the Rhode Island School of Design, and currently lives with his husband in Los Angeles.

ENDPAPER NOTE

"I'm not sure that anybody thinks about endpaper except publishers, and probably not more than 1800 people in the United States have ever heard the word 'endpaper,'" E.B. White wrote to his editor, the visionary Ursula Nordstrom, before insisting that the endpapers of his *Charlotte's Web* be beautiful. The loveliest of books are touched by the author's thoughtfulness and care in every detail.

A Velocity of Being borrows its endpapers from one of the most imaginative details an author ever slipped into a book.

In 1759, Laurence Sterne began composing *The Life and Opinions of Tristram Shandy, Gentleman*—a seven-volume novel that would take him a decade to complete and would revolutionize the art of storytelling. Midway through the third volume, he placed a single marbled page—a shock of swirling color, strange and beautiful, against the black-and-white of the book. Sterne himself considered it the "motley emblem" of his work, imbued with meaning open to interpretation but never fully penetrable. It was a small revolution—aesthetically, because the craft of marbling, developed in the Middle East, was a curious novelty in mid-18th-century Britain; conceptually, because the fluid dynamics of the dyes make each marbling unique and irreplicable, like each reading of a book, colored by the dynamics we bring to it, the swirl of its meaning co-created by author and reader.

Years ago, when *A Velocity of Being* was still an untitled baby of a project, my then-partner and I had the fortune of acquiring one of the handful of surviving first editions of *Tristram Shandy* at the New York Antiquarian Book Fair. As I marveled at this centuries-old marbled page, I knew instantly that it would make the perfect endpaper—aesthetically and symbolically, a "motley emblem" of the joy and ever-swirling meaning of literature itself. — Maria Popova

A NOTE ON THE TYPE

The letters in this book are set in Miller Text, a typeface designed by Matthew Carter and released in 1997. Carter was inspired by types from Scottish foundries of the 19th century.

Authors' biographies are set in Brandon Text, designed by Hannes von Döhren and released in 2012. Hannes was influenced by the geometric-style sans serif faces that were popular during the 1920s and 30s.

The title on the cover of the book is set in Ogg, a typeface designed by Lucas Sharp and Greg Gazdowicz, and released in 2013. Ogg is inspired by the hand lettering of 20th-century book designer and calligrapher Oscar Ogg.

All proceeds from the sale of this book will go to support
the public libraries of New York City.

Abundant thanks to Clément Bénech, Anna Celada, and Kate
Finney for collecting materials and maintaining archives over
many years. Much thanks as well to Marc Drumwright and
Julie Kwon for jumping in at the last minute.

www.enchantedlion.com

First published in 2018 by Enchanted Lion Books
67 West Street, 317A, Brooklyn, NY 11222

A CIP record is on file with the Library of Congress

ISBN 978-1-59270-228-2

Printed in China by R. R. Donnelley Asia Printing Solutions

Third Printing

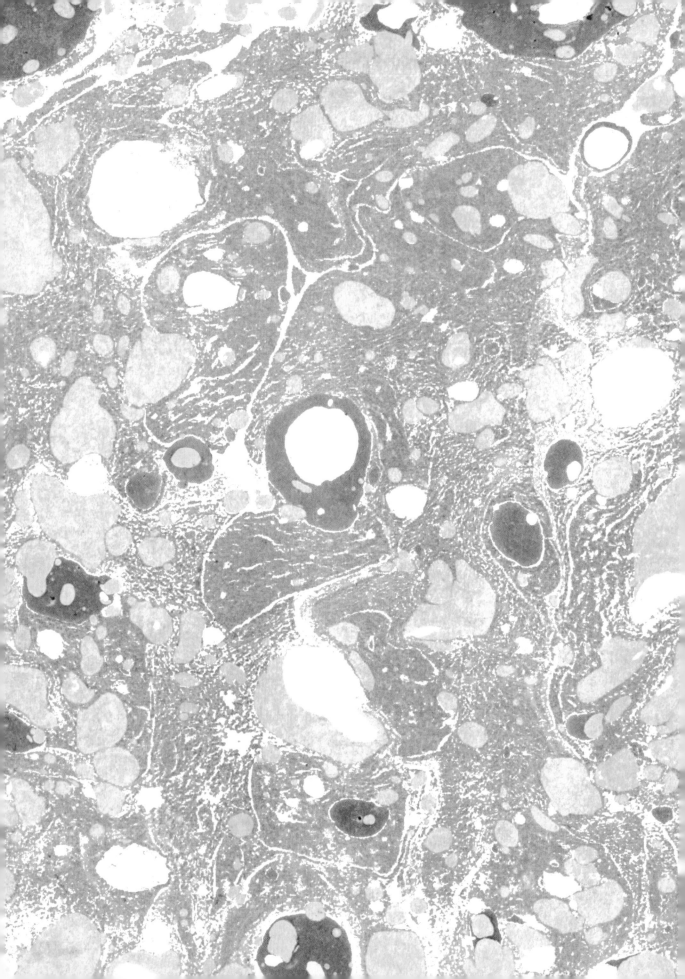